LEE VALLEY POEMS

(A PROJECT OF POEMS & TRANSLATION)

李河谷的诗

（一个诗与翻译的项目）

Yang Lian was one of the original Misty Poets who reacted against the strictures of the Cultural Revolution. Born in Switzerland, the son of a diplomat, he grew up in Beijing and began writing when he was sent to the countryside in the 1970s. On his return co-founded the influential literary magazine *Jintian* (*Today* – now published in exile in Scandinavia). His work was criticised in China in 1983 and formally banned in 1989. He has lived in exile since 1989, when he organised memorial services for the dead of Tiananmen while in New Zealand. After spells in Australia, Germany and the USA, he settled in London.

Translations of his poetry include three collections with Bloodaxe, *Where the Sea Stands Still* (1999), a Poetry Book Society Recommended Translation, *Concentric Circles* (2005), and *Lee Valley Poems* (2009), as well as *Riding Pisces: Poems from Five Collections* (Shearman, 2008), a compilation of earlier work.

YANG LIAN

LEE VALLEY POEMS

BLOODAXE BOOKS

Copyright © Yang Lian 2009
Translations copyright © Yang Lian, Polly Clark, Antony Dunn,
Jacob Edmond, W.N. Herbert, Pascale Petit, Fiona Sampson, Arthur Sze,
and Brian Holton & Agnes Hung-Chong Chan, as acknowledged.

ISBN: 978 1 85224 834 5

First published 2009 by
Bloodaxe Books Ltd,
Highgreen,
Tarset,
Northumberland NE48 1RP.

www.bloodaxebooks.com
For further information about Bloodaxe titles
please visit our website or write to
the above address for a catalogue.

Supported by
**ARTS COUNCIL
ENGLAND**

Cover design: Neil Astley & Pamela Robertson-Pearce.

Printed in Great Britain by
Bell & Bain Limited, Glasgow, Scotland.

TRANSLATORS

[PC/YL]	Polly Clark *with Yang Lian*
[AD/YL]	Antony Dunn *with Yang Lian*
[JE]	Jacob Edmond
[WNH/YL]	W.N. Herbert *with Yang Lian*
[BH]	Brian Holton
[BH/AC]	Brian Holton & Agnes Hung-Chong Chan
[PP/YL]	Pascale Petit *with Yang Lian*
[FS/YL]	Fiona Sampson *with Yang Lian*
[AS/YL]	Arthur Sze *with Yang Lian*

ACKNOWLEDGEMENTS

Acknowledgements are due to the editors of the following publications where some of these translations first appeared: *Agenda* ('Valley and the End: A Story'), *Brand* ('Another Decade, Hudson River'), Gulf Coast ('Memorial to a Tree at the Street Corner'), *Poetry London* ('Another Decade, Hudson River', 'Brian Holton Travelling in New Zealand', 'Ghost Sonatas' 'Stroller'), *Poetry Review* ('A wild goose speaks to me', 'Home', 'The Journey' and *The Stinging Fly* ('What Water Confirms', part 7). Polly Clark's co-translation of 'Where the River Turns' appeared in her collection *Take Me with You* (Bloodaxe Books, 2005).

This book is published with the assistance of a grant for translation costs from Arts Council England's Grants for the arts scheme funded by the National Lottery.

LOTTERY FUNDED

CONTENTS

A Wild Goose Speaks to Me

'There is no international, only different locals': my essay *The International inside the Local* is summed up by this statement. What is "local"? Are its contents geographical, psychological, historical, language-based or even linguistics-based? How can a poet write a poem entitled 'The archaeology of the now'? The poet archaeologist, as if uncovering layer upon layer of earth, seeks the ever more deeply hidden self, and the poem, like an archaeological manual, records the experience of excavating ever deeper within one site. And for us, the depth we reach through the process of comparing poem with poem (especially with the poet's earlier work) confirms the value and the status of that poem, to the point that "local" doesn't at all signify a specific site, but must point to all sites, as being the ability of the poet to excavate his own self. The poet says, 'Give me a single breath, and I will grow roots, penetrate the soil, probe shingle and magma, and hear the sea through every artery and vein of groundwater, sharing the voyage of every navigator since the dawn of time.'

So, on this summer night, through the open window of my bedroom, direct to my eardrum comes the cry of a wild goose, shattering the dark green glass-like silence of London, and in the timbre of every chilly honk a secret world is uncovered. What I want to know is, what is that's touching my heart so much?

Is it this city of London? It's one of the countless foreign towns I've drifted through. Originally, as with other temporary resting places, the Stoke Newington postcode, still unmemorised, then discarded, shrunken, fixed and buried in my CV, became just a line of letters no one paid any attention to. But against all expectation, I went on living there. Some years after the city had become gradually familiar, as "of their own accord" my eyes began to look for the last apple on the branches of the same apple tree each November: I suddenly realised that my relationship with London had changed. It no longer rubbed shoulders as it passed me by, but it had come to a halt, to turn into the first "local" I had had since I left China. Even stranger than simple peripatetic exile, this superficial standstill doubly demonstrated life cannot help but move.

Was it through writing the collection *Lee Valley Poems* in London that these external places are converted into my inner self, to become part of the 'I' of the text? In fact, even the word "exile" is empty: if it weren't for the substance of poetry, we wouldn't even be worthy of our own experience. The blood-dripping funnel image which I had to create, comes to include the garden I look down on from my kitchen window as well as all the gardens that sink deep in the autumn rain. The line 'confirming the wind goes away also along itself', which I had to find, comes to express the street before us, blown with dry fallen leaves, as well as all the streets the wanderer's road has followed. As the psychological rollover of time is folded into geographical space, these images become more local the more they point to the theme of human 'placelessness'. Apart from a line of poetry, we have nowhere to exist.

Or again, are China and Chinese language what the cry of the wild goose summons? At present, I jokingly called them 'my own foreign country' and 'my foreign mother-tongue'. Since long ago, fleeing from home has been seen in China as the cruellest experience that anyone could undergo (and please note that the expression 'flee from home' literally translates as 'turning your back on the old well [of home]'); so the wild goose that follows the seasons north and south as it migrates become the emblem of the homeless wanderer. Those skeins of geese which form the Chinese character 人 [person] are always going home. Yet the sight-line of those who watch them fly away can never return home. Skimming through the ancient poetry of the Tang dynasty [618-960 AD], we see the wild goose as practically synonymous with heartbreak and longing. Witness lines such as these: 'Returning wild geese enter an alien sky', or 'When the wild geese return they bring many letters from home' by Wang Wei [701-761 AD]; 'When the wild goose is lost in blue sky' or 'The wild geese guide the sorrowful heart far away' by Li Bai [701-762 AD]; 'The heart flies into extinction with the wild geese' or 'Leaves fall as the wild geese go south' by Meng Haoran [689-740 AD]; 'On the autumn frontier the wild goose cries once' or 'When will the wild geese bring a letter?' by Du Fu [712-770 AD]. Du Fu, who was by far the most adept at describing the hardships of the wandering life, has a poem simply titled A Solitary Wild Goose, which contains the couplet 'Who pities a shard of shadows / lost to each other inside many-layered clouds?': long ago, he set down a definitive description of the situation I which I find myself today.

Classical Chinese poetry emphasises allusion, which, via the means of 'inter-modularity'[1] allows all tradition to be contained in a newly written text. With the cry of the wild goose, I am drawn into the Tang dynasty at the instant of hearing, making Lee valley's waters flow twelve hundred years upstream – and isn't that a kind of 'distance'? or actually, a 'nearness' pressing toward to me? I could almost greet all the Du Fus as they hurry past the corner of the street huddled in their long scholars' gowns, just as I greet my well-known and familiar neighbours.

Poetry includes all of that. Here 'distant' and 'deep' mean the same thing. The poet may travel far, but never really leave the autochthonous ground of his own inner self. The world slips by him like an abstract setting, and the distance between its fluctuating changes exists only in the direction of the internal inquiry. The poet's standards shift as the poetry imperceptibly moves them towards the vertical. That is to say, so-called 'depth' solely indicates the poet's comprehension of existence, as seen in his writing: Heidegger's statement that 'All great thinkers have spoken the same thought' is pointing out this idea about 'existence'. The value and the joy of poetry can be described as fishing in the deep sea of existence. In comparison with the substance of this, the pursuit of changes in subject matters, novelty of form, individuality of style, even political correctness or identity games – these are all shadows, aims which are too superficial and which will weaken the meaning of the poetry. Sticking with 'the human condition', a poem contains a definite set of concentric circles: Tang poetry, China, foreign countries, London, the Lee Valley, my tiny study, the specific moment of writing a word, the non-time implied by the tenselessness characteristic of the Chinese verb, these are all in the 'I'. When they are no longer merely knowledge, but have become the poet's 'thought', then a poem has connected with the energy source of itself.

I know that today, when the post-modern is so pervasive, there are dangers in discussing or even raising the issue of 'depth'. But today's reality is tense, full of the smell of gunpowder even more than was the cold war. Today's art theory has been able to stand before the sediment of the twentieth century and reflect on its superstitious faith in novelty of from. Today's philosophical question – the precise antonym for 'today' – is just this: how can we abolish the mirage of time, and face anew the emptiness and darkness which have been eternally co-existent with human nature? In a word, the energy to do so comes from the awareness of the predicament. If an inopportune or out-of-style idea can continue to create good poetry, then that is the nature of poetry.

I didn't know the wild goose that cried to me on that summer night, but I have heard in it the skeins of wild geese that have flown over every poet in every era, and they have never migrated from that clear and melodic voice.

SECTION ONE

Short Poems

第一部分：短诗

在河流转弯处　（一）

这儿　油亮的水面上发育着另一个身子
这油腻腻的蓝色两翼　扇着
从未真正抵达的秋天

从来都是秋天　河流转弯处
季节再次与你相关
注视　把眼睛无情抛弃

没有什么久远的事　一张长椅
深深陷进自己沉思的天性
一个河面遍布迎向逆光的小小断崖
波浪滑过象只瓷器微微爆裂
又粘合了　蒲棒们的花纹从水上
掼到岸上　而岸　还在自你内心移出

空气中激动死者的鲜味儿
响应一个冷艳的指挥的手势

在河流转弯处　（二）

这儿　水平平铺开两个方向的倒叙
在河流转弯处　一个人撤出年龄

才拥有许多刻进椅背的名字
阳光撒出一下午眩目的地理学

另一些停过这里的体温回忆着你
另一片干了的水迹把傍晚

概括成吐出的　血污的
两个死亡中乌鸦朝此刻斜视

划船的女性手臂朝两个终点最后冲刺
天鹅被看不见的饥饿逼着

亲近河的肉香　你坐在鱼刺顶端
两个方向上的过去都是空的

Where the River Turns

I

here   a form opens on the sheen of the water
two oily blue wings   fanning out
an autumn that never truly reaches you

an autumn that is here forever   where the river turns
the season again becomes part of you
your eyes   abandoned by all they see

no single thing lasts for long   a bench
sinks deep into its own nature   lost in thinking
the river is carved with tiny cliffs against the light
the ripples splinter like porcelain
and grow together again   the reeds' candle-hearts are a shadow-pattern
thrown against the bank   and the bank   drifts out from your heart

the sky's fresh scent excites the dead
as if answering to a conductor's cold and beautiful gesture

II

here   water spreads from two directions   two flashbacks
where the river turns   a man turns away from the passage of time

and the names dug into the bench's back become his
sunlight turns away from the afternoon's dazzling geography

the warmths of other bodies which sat here remember you
the stains of dried-out waters record the dusk

spewed-out   bloodied
the shuttered eye of a crow stares into this moment   from two deaths

the arms of women in a rowing boat drive toward two finishes
swans forced by invisible hunger

slip in beside the river's scented flesh   you exist at the point of a fish bone
the pasts in two directions are both empty

在河流转弯处 （三）

这儿 一枚鸟头找到它自己的沼泽
去腐烂 骷髅雪白而精巧
如一个放弃飞翔的思想
日子总能让你陷进去
齐眉的甜蜜水声中 听觉
本身就是一个洞穴
河拉开一架真丝屏风
盛过天空的身体都变换着光速
湿再次与你相关 却与水无关
湿湿的窗口从河底漏下 野树丛
吸去心跳和空荡荡的眼眶
蓝的暴力像块颅骨倒扣着
从未真正抵达的远方
从来在逼近脚下
书架上一只小水晶盒子灌满死后
瀑布似的距离又把你抠出来

III

here   a bird hunted down a marsh
for a grave   its skull snow white and exquisite
like a thought that has given up flying
the day let you sink below its surface
the sweet sound of water immersed you to your brow
hearing became a cave
the river opened a silk screen
the body that spooned the sky now changes at the speed of light
wetness becomes part of you again   but it is a stranger to water
a wet window sieved from the bottom of the river   the wild bush
sucks the beating heart and empty eye socket away

the sky's blue violence like a skullcap placed down

the distant place that can never be reached
forever advances through wings and feet
death is sealed in a crystal box on the bookshelf
the far waterfall hooks you back into air

在河流转弯处　（四）

这儿　河转身　冻红的灌木转身
苇叶被修剪的响声　剪下仍不够黑暗的
星星转到看不见的另一侧
都是人形

复眼们繁殖在天上
又一片城市灯火　从你内脏里浮出
水面纵横的裂缝犹如籍贯

你刚刚被改写的
不得不接受的这一个
　　　　　这场吱吱叫的雨
从未真正打进任何一夜
从来都是最可怕的物种

地平线转回来　你有这么多白茫茫的水

推开水中已不抓什么的手
停顿再次与皮肤相关　满河谷的珠光
给你一个这儿　斟满数不清的哪儿
给喝醉一个形象　今夜高地上
谁戴着金面具　海鸥倒映看不见的海
折断的白十字　在头上钉牢了

　　　　一滴雨蜇着宇宙
涮洗　一对被摘掉的聋耳
捱过这条肉质的边界吧

18

IV

here   the river turns   the ice-pink bush turns
hear the reed cutter   cutting back what is not dark enough
stars turn to the side we cannot see
all of them in human shape

compound eyes reproduce across the sky
the vast expanse of city lights   surfaces from deep inside your body
cracks criss-cross the water as if from an origin

that has just been rewritten for you
the one you cannot help but accept

                this swarming rain
that can never reach a real night
is forever the most terrified species

the horizon turns away   you have endless blank waters

the water waves like a drowned hand

stillness becomes part of your skin again   the pearl light is full of the river
it gives you *here*   pours to the brim the countless *where*s
it gives drunkenness a form   on the hill in the darkness
it wears a golden mask   seagulls mirror the invisible sea
like broken white crosses   nailed above your head

                a drop of rain stings the universe
wash   this pair of ears, torn off and deaf
bear your burden   this transgressed boundary of flesh

[PC/YL]

19

云

它们的时间是否也像一大块粘粘的血污
它们的乐谱架　遮着天蓝的演奏着
慢板和小快板擦洗一座阳台
河谷倒扣下来　风声灌满剧场
舞台上遍布急急回家的

无家的　它们的孤独捻着一只玻璃眼珠
它们的头都飞离了雪白荒凉的颈椎
虚拟的桨手　梦见近得可怕的岸

是个房间　出租衣柜里花朵纷纷褪色
午餐穿上岛的时速　曝着
盘子上一群猛兽从左边跃向右边
被切开就像被误认为停留过
它们用每个剧目更换一种方言
和血肉　菜谱中的蝴蝶翅膀片片嚼碎
窗口转暗　偷渡另一条边界

借一个地址　去加深一封信的忧郁吧

这忘了寄信者的　不停涂改水面的
一个戏剧性把世界缩减成
摒住呼吸的　想抹去就抹去的形象
它们越过自己的远　卷起帷幕
接近了生命中隐秘的部分

20

Clouds

Is time a big blob of sticky blood for them too?
Their music-stands   screen the sky-blue performer
Lento and *Allegretto* scrub and rinse a balcony
The river valley turns upside-down   and the sound of wind fills the theatre
its stage crowded   with people hurrying home

the homeless   Their loneliness fingers the glassy eyeball
their heads have flown from the snow-white, desolate tips of their spines
they pretend to be rowers who dream the bank is terrifyingly close –

A room   flowers fading on a rented wardrobe
lunch going at island speed   Glimpses
Wild animals jumping from side to side   above your plate
                          Being cut up: just like the illusion of standing still
They change dialect and incarnation
with each drama   Fragment by fragment the butterfly-wings on the menu
                                          are chewed up
the window goes dark for a scene-change   steals across another border

Now borrow an address   to deepen the gloom with a letter –

stage directions don't remember who posted it   keep changing the
                                          water's surface
shrink the world
into images that catch the breath   that can be erased at will
They reach beyond their own remoteness   raising the curtain
to approach the inner life

[FS/YL]

21

散步者

水下的金鱼是否会歌唱一座城市的兴衰
河边一排钻研羽毛的天鹅
是否在刻划 揽镜自照的少女
风声灌满了他散步的自我
　　　被黑暗中一条街领着
到这片沼泽里 脚陷下一寸深
绿漫出堤岸熟读冬天的无奈
一场雨后 草叶破碎的膝盖到处跪着
一块云虚构一次日蚀
他在地平线远眺中忽明忽暗
　　　繁衍有只雁整整叫过的一夜
到这个遗忘里
感觉被河谷温柔地吞下去
感觉自己已变成河谷 一株枯柳
爆炸的金色 投掷一只不停分娩天空的子宫
　　　听木栅栏在风中呼啸
　　　被钉死才拦住日子
到达水和血湿漉漉的相似性
沉溺等在这儿 小酒馆絮絮叨叨的未来
锁着门 一城市的他端着冷了的杯子
　　　像个被栽种的呼吸
走得更远 埋进老铁桥的骸骨
不可能再远 大丛暗红锈蚀的灌木
逼入窗户 阳光鬼魅地一亮
提示他头上定居的阴沉沉的水位
　　　哈死的风景到了
　　　黑暗中拆散的
　　　　　孤悬的台阶到了

Stroller

Whether the golden fish sing about the rise and fall of the city or not
a line of swans on the riverbank study the book of their feathers
whether they model girls with mirrors or not
the stroller's self is filled completely by the sound of the wind
    led by a pitch-dark street
towards this stretch of marshland   where feet sink in an inch
the banks overflow with green which knows winter's weakness only too well
after the rain   the grassblades kneel on broken knees
one cloud invents an eclipse
the horizon watches him abruptly change between light and dark
    breeding a night
    in which a wild goose calls him continuously
towards this act of forgetting
feeling softly swallowed by the valley
feeling he has already become the valley   an empty willow
which throws out a womb in a golden explosion endlessly giving birth to the sky
    listening to the wooden fence shout in the wind
    so nailed to death it stops the day
he arrives at the shared wetness of water and blood
where drowning waits   the chattering future a little bar
with a locked door   he is the entire city holding a stone cold cup
    as though planted, panting
walking further to be buried in the skeleton of an old iron bridge
walking impossibly further   rusty blood-red bushes
burst through his window   ghost-like sunlight appears once
revealing the swollen dark water-level settled over his head
    the drowned landscape is here
    in the dark the separated
                lonely hanging step is here

[WNH/YL]

河谷的姓氏

四次见到枝头一枚最后的苹果
你离这姓氏就不远了 四场
下了整个冬天的雨连成一条虚线
慢慢剥光你的衣服 找到
一个黄昏认领的冻红的焦点
公园里修剪整齐的柏树忍着形式
水淋淋的云层收藏烂掉的果肉
寒风中 乌鸦被它的世界语染得更黑

你却听懂了 脱尽叶子的链条上
一只锁住的苹果在荡回来
孤儿似的香像粒深陷的籽
埋在河谷下 喊一声雨就落了
喊到你的乳名 你的血型就变了
鸟巢高高的单间卧室浸透水
一滴漫过一生 在你肺里
被继承的命运撒着雪花

24

The Valley's Surname

The fourth year you see the very last apple on the branch
then you are close to this surname   four rains
each one lasting all winter – make a dotted line
that slowly strips you   seeking
the ice-red focus adopted by twilight
In the park the harshly pruned cypresses endure their shape
swollen clouds gather rotten fruit-flesh
Inside the biting wind   a crow is dyed even blacker by its esperanto

yet you understand   on the leafless chain of a branch
a padlocked apple sways bringing you back
its abandoned-baby scent of a deeply sunk seed
buried under the valley   when it calls you once – rain falls
but when it calls your pet-name   your blood-type changes
then in the high single bedroom of a waterlogged bird's nest
one drop drowns your whole life   in your lungs
a fatal heritage scatters snowflakes

[PP/YL]

旅程

一 .

雁叫的时候我醒着　雁在
万里之外叫　黑暗在一夜的漩涡中
如此清越

河弯过去　口渴的人
臆想一杯水墨绿色的直径
陷进玻璃的翅尖冷冷扇着冷冷发脆

沙漏　为沿街每一幢房子下锚
雨后的轮胎撕开长长的绷带

我听见我身体里那些船
在碰撞　龙骨们挤进干裂的一根
雁叫时　粘在耳膜上的城市
悬在别处飞　一种轻如残骸的地理学

二 .

　　　水是没有意义的
河弯过去　风摩擦干了的船底
老鼠们喜欢攀登这付铁架子
锈腥味儿　象漂亮的鱼刺
月光漆着一个弧度　死者上妆的脸
安静得像只木头子宫丢在岸边
离水声一点远　离沙石小路一点远
离星座间摆脱了方向的舵一点远
收拢的桨像累了的疑问
死死缠在轴上

　　　水是没有意义的
但水的瓷　烧绘出港口的图案
时间带来回忆的主题
一条被悬空架起的船能回忆些什么
除了一个听觉　水一样细密缝合着
除了一只铃　摇响就在删去
雕花的耳朵　候鸟逡巡
　　　　而地球错开一步
光年交叉中圆圆的巢
再也找不到　谁驶过哪条河

26

The Journey

1

I wake when the wild goose calls, a cry
thousands of miles away, piercing
night's whirlpool.

The river turns. A parched child
thinks of a glass's inky rim
and wingtips sunk in cold crystal.

Night's hourglass anchors my house to the street.
After rain, tyres tear long bandages from the road.

I hear the boats in my body
jostling against each other, their keels fused.
When the wild goose cries, the city stuck to my eardrum
flies elsewhere, a geography light as a wreck.

2

      Water tells nothing.
The river turns. Wind rasps the hulls.
Rats love climbing the davit struts.
Rust sticks in my throat like a fish-bone.
Moonlight casts a lunar arc, painting a corpse's face,
quiet as a wooden womb thrown on the bank,
just by the lapping water, the gravel,
just by the rudder which has escaped all bearings among the stars,
the oars drawn in like tired questions
bound in a stranglehold around the axle.

      Water tells nothing, but
on the water-surface the marina's glaze is fire-painted.
The clock ticks backwards –
what can a boat cradled by air remember
except water's embroidery,
except to be a bell, ringing to delete
my coiled ear, the ceaseless migrations.
      But earth stalls.
The light-years woven around its nest
no longer know who sails on what river.

水 烧结成这块摔不碎的瓷
早碎了 隔开一夜已隔开许多夜
隔着酷爱作曲的历史

　　　　水是没有意义的 因而
升起潜望镜的恐怖
醒在一艘弃船里 醒着看
天上亿万条轨道高擎一朵朵荷花
都关紧粉红色 喃喃而说时
被一个无力怀旧的语法抓着
铁的器官屈服于内部的空
还能撑多久 当一条鱼精选氧气里的毒
还试图辨认什么 这一眨不眨的眼前
黎明无须过渡 黎明已徜游在别处
刺骨的美学 离孤独
一点儿远

雁叫的国度是一个坐标
在水下 哪个死者能继续昨晚中断的旅程

　　　三.

圆心 隐身张望的文本
把我变成又一页初稿
圆 漂在鬼魂笔迹里的床
被水暴露也被水取消

雁真叫过吗 或一夜深邃到非时间
雁弯弯割断的脖子
越怕听越易于被唤出

听觉比喻地貌 黑暗
比喻一种扣留我的物质
城市的流体溅出一枝桃花
否决地平线的 还是震耳欲聋的心跳声

大脑比喻星空 床沿
比喻一条崩紧的船舷
尖叫囚入一滴雨 梦的万有引力
从它们的万里之外彼此思念
都在圆上 都被还没写出的驱逐着

弯回此地

28

Water sinters into shatterproof porcelain
long broken, fissioning every night,
shattering my past, which so loves to invent.

Water tells nothing, therefore
in my abandoned boat, I can't raise the periscope
to peep at the sky where billions of orbits
clasp their lotus-suns. They close their corals, whisper
in a language which has no past tense, no nostalgia.
Their iron organs implode.
How long can we survive, when fish seek the poison in oxygen?
What more can we possibly find in an unblinking eye?
Dawn won't arrive. Dawn has swum elsewhere,
its beauty cuts me to the quick.

The wild geese's cries are an underwater co-ordinate.
What corpse can continue the journey ended last night?

3

At the circle's centre, a text secretly watches me
draft another page.
My bed circles – floating in a ghost script
revealed then unravelled by water.

Did the wild geese really cry, or is this night too adrift
for their arched and chopped necks?
The more afraid I am to listen, the easier they're summoned.

Their call transforms the landscape; darkness
transforms my flesh;
the city's hydromechanics splash out a branch of peach-blossom.
A hammering heartbeat still withholds the horizon.

My mind is a starry sky; my bed-edge
a starboard –
a scream locked in a raindrop, the pull of dreams
longing for each other over thousands of miles
all in the circle, driven out by what isn't yet written

only to circle back to here.

[PP/YL]

家（一）

欠缺的那只猫在家具间行走
给雨天一块白　瓶子洗净了
器官们璀璨地悬在体外
每只有一对叮当作响的南北极
用欠缺的磁力线顶着冰雪
又一小时　把你和我移入一艘
飞船　手拉手　惊叫　闭眼
幻想能在疯了的星空中稳住

家（二）

你亮而细的鼾声远远围拢
夜　有根剪下来精工雕琢的彗尾
这房子　浮在水上就追随
水的形状　衬着磷光持续发黑
衬着秒针的舌头卷走了世界

诗人需要一只笼子　不小于
我被容忍的愚蠢　墙换了又换
而一幅画倚着虚空　定居在风中
琴声搁进宛如旧书的一件往事
错得可爱　非错不可才迁徙成诗艺

灯有只蛾子的自我
光速在肉里猛烈地醒着
追上地平线时享受一顿湛蓝的晚餐
还泛着油漆香　撕掉皮肤就撕掉
你和我　和下一个订制的早晨

Home

1

The cat who ought to be here strolls between the furniture,
supplying a blank to the rainy day.   Bottles are being washed –
organs hanging shining outside the body.
Each has a ringing pair of north and south poles
binding ice and snow with absent lines of magnetic force.
Another hour moves you and me into
the space-craft   holding hands   screaming   eyes closed.
Imagine being secured in the mad star-sky.

2

Your thin shining snores   circle far away.
Night has a delicately-carved cut-off comet's tail,
this house floats on water, following
the form of water   continually darkening against the phosphorescence,
sweeping the world away with the second-hand's tongue.

A poet needs a cave   no smaller than
his intolerable stupidity,   the walls change and change again
and a painting hung on the emptiness   makes itself at home in the wind.
The sound of music is put into the old book of the past:

A lovely *miniature*,   it must be a *miniature* to move toward the art of the pen.
The lamp takes over a moth's self,
the speed of light wakes violently in flesh.
Enjoying an azure dinner, catching up with the horizon,
still smelling the fragrance of the paint: to rip off skin means to rip off
you and me   and the next made-to-measure morning.

[FS/YL]

STOKE NEWINGTON　即景

阳光象谎言那么美　一点点增强
街上的灵车闪烁预约的亮度

桃花把墓地带在身上
死者们嘴里　满含薄薄的花瓣

枝头的三月　世界形成于
女孩耳垂后边钻心的某一点

你的路口上　回忆嗅着风
你的风摇荡复制芳香的方程式

中年　看不见起点也看不见尽头
犹如下课铃被无限拉长了

刺耳的一刻　梨树身穿藏青色制服
没完没了拥出小学校门口

水面颤抖如马驹油腻的皮肤
你的抚摸又温柔又粗暴

一双手被空气的玻璃分解
许多一生摸到雨珠密密麻麻的盲文

寒意涌来时　两端都弯向地下
这路口对称于你的两个末日

色情得象件粘合如新的瓷器
词的惊人在越老越鲜艳

刚亮起又暗了　天空卷起蓝图
雨丝平行的斜线织出雨声的几何学

Stoke Newington Scene

sunlight as beautiful as lies   strengthens bit by bit
the brightness of the hearse's twinkling appointment on the street

peach blossom carries the graveyard on its back
the mouths of the dead   are full of flimsy petals

in the March of branch ends   the world forms
a certain point in the middle of the piercing at the back of a girl's earlobe

at your intersection   sniffing the wind recollect
your wind sways reproducing a fragrant equation

midway through life   one can see neither the starting point nor the end
like the bell at the end of class extended without limit

an ear-piercing moment   pear trees wear uniforms that conceal their green
endlessly surging out of the primary-school gates

the water's surface trembles like the oily hide of a foal
your caresses are gentle and brutal

a pair of hands is broken up by the glass of the air
many spend a lifetime feeling the dense braille of rain beads

when the chilly air gushes forth   both ends bend toward the ground
this intersection stands in symmetry with both your final days

pornographically resembling a piece of chinaware glued together to look new
the surprise of words grows older more intense

what just lit up again darkens   the sky rolls up its blueprint
the oblique parallel lines of the rain's threads weave the geometry of the sound
of rain

[JE]

纪念一棵街角上的树

昨夜　我的诗移到街角上
扮演一棵树　挥舞
鬼魂那样猛转过脸来的小白花

踮起脚尖叫　空中遍布
闪烁晶莹的踝骨
唐代像盏灯候地被拧亮

已经第几年　沿着红砖墙
拐弯就是故国　枝头
熟悉的血又找到替身

泼出成吨的水银色
不再怕凋谢　自涮洗春天的
一夜　树桩上袅袅的电锯声

Memorial to a Tree at the Street Corner

last night   my poem moved to the street corner
enacted a tree   waved
small white flowers that suddenly turned their faces like ghosts

screaming on tiptoe   permeated the air
ankle bones sparkled like crystals
the Tang dynasty like a lantern suddenly switched on

already it's been so many years   along a red brick wall
I turned a corner it was the old country   at branch tip
familiar bloodshed finds again its stand-in

throws out tons of quicksilver colours
but I am no longer scared of shriveling   since a spring night
washed away   at the tree stump the lingering sound of an electric saw

[AS/YL]

个人地理学

　　　　　别人看不见
比高地更高　有乌鸦白茫茫的领空
公园抖动它的绿　抖着
子宫壁上的肌肉　分娩
花瓣哭成一片的春天
手掌上满载故事的地图
斜斜织入这条街　什么也不说
就变了　树木的密码锁
一拨一个去年　再拨
压死的鸟鸣都跃回枝头
水耽于幻想　万物的孤独
嵌在一枚人形的图钉上
别人看不见　阳光锤打中
你无知地跨进这个下午
跟着黑暗的指南

Personal Geography

                        Others can not see
the blank airspace of crows higher than the hill
the park convulsing its green   convulsing
the womb-wall muscle   giving birth
to spring cried out by the petals in their expanse
    The map of your palm holds all of the stories
weaves slantwise into this street   says nothing
but has changed   the combination lock of the trees
spins back one past year   and spins again
and all the birdsong crushed to death flips back into the branches
water indulges its own fantasies   the loneliness of all things
nailed by a hook in human form
    Others can not see   under the hammering sun
you walk unknowing into this afternoon
following a guidebook of darkness

[AD/YL]

空中的月夜

十五个小时的月亮在我左边
总在左边　机翼的裸体迎着黑暗

十五个被拉长的椭圆形
与时间无关　回头　满目你的冰雪

在升高　离别是朵盛开的奇花
用变大的回声吮含那只小铃

月光覆盖我　性交后的睡眠覆盖云
世界在哪儿　没人飞出此夜

哦　别停　别掉出一条河谷
的银色　保持匀速　这就是死亡

Moonlit Night in the Sky

fifteen hours of moon on my left
always on my left   the inner body of the airplane's wing greets the darkness

fifteen ovals that have been stretched out
unconnected to time   look back   your pure snow white fills my view

rising now   parting is a rare flower in full bloom
suck that little bell with a mounting echo

the moonlight covers me   sleep after sex covers the clouds
where is the world   nobody flies out of this night

oh   don't stop   don't drop one thread of river valley
silver   maintain an even speed   this is death

[JE]

鬼魂奏鸣曲

一．海与河

跨出栅栏就是大海
而两条鱼的克星 还要
一刹那更多的黑暗

跨出栅栏了 波浪的摇椅
摇着悬崖的突兀
每过一夜就再升高一点

他们的肉体
与脚下一阵阵涛声押韵
溢满他们的盲目

每个小小洞穴都湿淋淋的
每次呼吸都没有岸
他们彼此的楔形地带

彼此嵌入
咸腥的舔食在海面上漂流
礁石间一点灯火在哪个世纪

一亮 大海漏进手心
记忆有河水的本地口音
悬崖夜夜升高 崩塌已追上鸟翅了

栅栏之外 他们
偶然停在哪儿 就留在那儿
任一股黑潮从内心涌出．

Ghost Sonatas

1 *Ocean and River*

Beyond the fence there's only ocean
but the cursed fish-star still sucks
more darkness from this moment.

Beyond the fence, surging waves
shake the sheer cliff.
Every night they rear higher.

Our bodies rhyme
with the pounding surf beneath our feet –
a blinding flood.

Every little hole is drenched.
Every breath is shoreless.
Our bodies' coastlines

wedge into each other.
We lick salt from the sea's skin.
In what century was that lamp among the rocks

lit? The sea swishes in our palms.
Memory has a river's tongue.
The cliff rises higher each night to collapse at the wings of birds.

Beyond the fence where we happened
to stop, we will always pause
to loose a black tide from our hearts.

二．乐曲 - 花园

他们能看见那针管
推着致命的液体
这床边的黑

被乐曲浮雕着
花园的轮廓在返回
会呻吟的蕊　鲜艳就是返回

耻骨湿润　旋转
音符一尾一尾游离磁带
注射到深处　烛光摇着无限远

鬼魂暴露在隘口上
鬼魂的演奏　只挑选
肉质的隘口

那自幽香中反复成形的
蹂躏一枚花瓣　四季满室萦绕
他们带着上路的每一夜

都和星座一样大
按下黑暗的循环键　再唱
但什么也不能延迟

但鬼魂灌溉的
鬼魂还热烈采摘着　挣脱
鳞　即兴的死又刷新即兴的生

42

2 *The Music-Garden*

Night's syringe
shoots a lethal dose
of darkness around our bed.

Carved by music,
the garden's contours are returning.
A gasping corolla bursts into colour.

Our wet crotches
wrench musical notes from the cassette. One after the other they float up –
injected to the hilt. A candle flickers in deep space.

A ghost appears in the narrow pass.
It has chosen only the narrow pass of flesh
for its performance,

an endlessly recurring fragrance,
petal-trampling – all the seasons conjured in our room.
Every night the ghost ushers in

is huge as a constellation.
We press the rewind key for darkness to sing again
but nothing can be put off.

That which we water
the ghost passionately plucks, releasing us
from our scales. An improvised death renews our improvised life.

[PP/YL]

河谷与终结：一个故事

一

日子没有区别　话说了又说
湿漉漉的天空一件雨衣下摆
雨声敲着老照片里的白木桌子
两杯残茶　数着整下午倒扣的椅子
我们的嘴　五十年来挂在墙上

二

到处都是结尾　当你不再读下去
水面蹿起亮度　当你缩手
不再抚摸一头野兽绚丽的斑纹
隔着天气的同一个名字
如对岸叫喊的　离你远去的绿

三

一棵梨树或一棵菩提　截停了阳台
一间春天的卧室满满裸出花朵
鸟儿闪着珠光孵了一地
从还让你流淌的触摸的方式
肉体认出前世的寒意

四

一块糖软化了老女人吱吱叫的骨骼
我们能眺望那机器　点点滴滴
漏着茶色　裹紧抱怨声
又裹紧乌云　邻桌上起源的时间
用一根肠子　递过来结束的甜蜜

五

粼粼涟漪在窗外等着
惨白的沙石路　我们走来
鱼类百万只圆睁的空眼窝
插着雨的筷子　圆心
受制于最温柔的距离

六

你合上书也就合上了岸
天鹅的凝视雕刻这场景
房子　铁桥　静静浮现
脚蹼一翻　水下片片橘红的落叶
访问者秘密粉碎了一朵云

The Valley and the End: A Story

1

The days blend into each other – we keep saying the same old things.
The sky is a raincoat with a dripping hem.
Rain taps on white tables in old photos
and on two cups of half-drunk tea. All afternoon we counted the upturned chairs.
Our mouths have hung from the wall for fifty years.

2

Everywhere is ending. When you stop reading,
light leaps from the water's pelt. When you pull back your hand,
no longer touching the beast's gorgeous stripes,
your name is the same but sealed off by the weather,
like that loud green on the far bank gradually departing.

3

A pear tree blocks the balcony
and its spring bedroom full of naked flowers.
On the grass, birds hatch opalescent light.
Our bodies accept the coldness of a past life
by the way they touch and this still makes you wet.

4

A sugar lump melts an old woman's squeaking bones –
we can watch her organism, drop by drop,
leaking tea, swathing her groans
in vapour. Time begins at the next table,
passes the sweetness of the end through our guts.

5

Fish-rings wait for us outside the window.
We walked over that pale gravel path
to where a million fish eye-socket circles
are pierced by chopsticks of rain – the circles' centres
choked by the softest diameter.

6

You close the book then close the riverbanks.
Swan-stares carve this view –
the house, the iron bridge, that silently emerge –
their paddling feet are russet leaves under the water's surface
where our presence secretly shatters a cloud.

七

潜回一只六岁的小小浴缸
才六岁　躯体已被血红的瀑布
砸开　加入亵渎的文字
更多的过去中空气更稀薄
潜回女孩眼里的　是裸露到底的诗

八

但不是爱情诗　谁想浪费时间
就谈论时间　我们　河谷的美味
听上弦月的失重的马蹄铁
在脸上溅满泥泞　所谓重逢
即命令自己陷下去

九

历史渐渐幽暗　模拟着我们的器官
一根旧灯丝分泌出一片薄暮
煤气管戳穿细细的指尖
喷出火苗　嘶嘶烧结五点钟
满天归鸟都各自被钉在针上

十

两个尽头　既非是又非不
面面相觑的尽头　握住同一只茶杯
取暖　此刻的你自上衣外溢
两个回忆的光速滑翔星际
一把黑伞　被孤单运行的断手擎着

十一

全部罪恶和幸福只因为活过
当我们坐在桌边　衬托水的白
察觉不到流动时已流走了
终点最不像海　雨掐灭一秒钟
就忘了我们有一个过去

十二

袒露的性　在天上急速凝成一个点
舔着　野鸭胸前一抹宝石绿
雾中的树真美　那老照片
蒙着月光　像公园邀你漫步
夜空极近　隐在身后　邀你纵情呻吟

7

Dive back into the six-year-old's bathtub.
Just six years old, the body, already smashed open
by a blood-red torrent, has become a dirty word,
the air made even thinner the further back time reels.
What dives back into the girl's eyes is raw poetry

8

but it's not love poetry. Why waste time
by talking about time? We are the valley's delicacies.
We listen to the weightless horseshoe of the crescent moon
splashing mud on our faces – so cold a reunion
forces us to sink even deeper.

9

History gradually darkens, replicating our organs.
An old filament secretes a film of twilight.
That gas ring pierces thin fingers,
the flames spurt, hissing five o'clock with a furnace roar –
the entire sky of homing birds, each one nailed to the clock's hour hand.

10

Two ends – either yes or no.
Two ends like two people face to face, holding up the same cup
to keep warm – a present tense you spill from your clothes.
Two memories glide between stars at the speed of light,
a black umbrella lifted by a disembodied hand orbits

11

all sorrow and joy – just to be alive.
While we sit at the table against the blankness of water,
water flows away unnoticed.
The end is never like the sea, rain snuffs out one second
then we forget our past.

12

Naked sex converges on one point in the sky,
licks the emerald breasts of wild ducks.
Trees in fog are truly beautiful. That old photo
bathed in moonlight is the park inviting you for a stroll.
The night sky is so close, hiding at your back, inviting you to moan fiercely.

[PP/YL]

霍布恩在新西兰旅行

街是一篇篇译文　当你走过
那空地　一座被拆除的老房子会显灵
一个海盐味儿的声音邀你

喝一杯　厨房里酿了十年的酸啤酒
我的灯亮了十年　我的海面
那棵摘不完的柠檬树伸到窗前
把沙滩染黑了　镶在诗稿边上
你译错一个字　一台老式绞干机
就转着　阳光拉出一匹白布
有的人疯了　有的人死了

星期日　远近的钉子在木头里砸着
山谷的绿都为笛子准备好
鸟爪下一个即将开始的雨季
天空转暗　云变成一只只死羊羔
野茴香嗅着谁的傍晚

我的　野猫似的目送就象迎接
或你的　分解成五十盏路灯的五十岁
象首叙事诗　架起通往老房子的桥
医院的星系比记忆只深一点儿
鬼魂开车掠过　瞥见墓地时
继续挪动海浪间一个岛的位置
要到桥那边　你得旅行三次
在译文里　在诗句里　在风景里

三倍的距离押着你返回
大海的亲属们又冷又黑召唤的血缘

真的母语没有词　就象母亲
早知道你也会望着山顶一片白雪气喘嘘嘘
或我　伏在无遮无掩的体内
学海鸥叫　朝眼前漆黑开阔的一夜叫
真的孤单在岩石棱角上挂满哨音
风来了　亡灵应声飞起

母亲早知道你还会错
孩子们扎进针叶林　该庆幸还能错
一张导游图查不到飞翔的老房子
一部过去的词典　被你随身带到这儿

Brian Holton Travelling in New Zealand

every street is a translation   as you walk by
the empty lot   the ghost of an old demolished building might manifest itself
the sound of the sea's salty smell invite you

to drink a glass   sour beer brewed ten years in the kitchen
my lamp has burned ten years   my sea's surface
the inexhaustible lemon tree reaching toward the window
dyeing the beach black   embedded in my draft poems
you mistranslated a word   so an old-fashioned mangle
turns   sunlight drawing out a length of white cotton
some have gone mad   some have died

Sunday   nails far and near banged into the wood
the valley's green all prepared for the flute
beneath bird claws the rainy season about to start
sky turns dark   every cloud turns into a dead lamb
wild fennel scenting someone's evening

my   wildcat eyes seeing you off like a welcome
or your   fifty years of age broken down into fifty streetlamps
like a narrative ballad   building a bridge towards the old house
a hospital's galaxy only a little deeper than memory
driving ghosts brush by   when they glimpse the graveyard
go on shifting the position of an island among waves
if you want to cross the bridge you must travel three times
in translation   in verse   and in the landscape

a threefold distance escorts you back
to the cold and black summoning blood ties of ocean's kin

the real mother-tongue has no words   like mother
long ago knew you would be panting towards the white snow of the summits
or me   hidden in a body open to all
learning the seagull's cry   crying to pitch-black night open before my eyes
true loneliness hung with the sound of whistling on rocky edges
the wind rises   soul of the dead rising with the sound

mother knew long ago you'd be wrong again too
kids pricked into coniferous woods   should rejoice they can still be wrong
old flying houses can't be found on a tourist map
a dictionary of the past   you brought here yourself

49

火山口等在吱吱响的木楼梯顶端
从未写成文字的　领你登上来
象母亲绘制的此刻
你脱掉借用的血肉
到无人处大醉一场

十年后我在伦敦　想着那杯酒
倒进大理石墓碑上一个匆匆的侧影

a volcanic crater waits at the top of the creaking wooden stairs
what's never been written in words   leads you up
like this moment mother painted
you take off borrowed flesh and blood
go where no one is to get good and drunk

ten years later I'm in London   thinking of that glass of wine
poured into the hurried silhouette on a marble headstone

[BH]

SECTION TWO

A Sequence

What Water Confirms

TRANSLATED BY BRIAN HOLTON
& AGNES HUNG-CHONG CHAN

第二部分：组诗

水肯定的

水肯定的

一

肯定　风也在沿着自己离去
遗传　姓氏里一片波光粼粼
秋天带着散步的人　慢跑的人
和十一月挂满树梢的铁铃
绕过街角　温暖
　　　　　　如别处的秋天

过去的所有形式舔向一道金黄的边缘

肯定　沿着他的下午
漆黑的柏油路在沉思这座房子
一只鸟头烂出了骷髅

　　　　"而水又西流，
　　　　　过大城曰……"

书上写了　一场雨来自深呼吸
注射进苹果的蓝　充满小学生的尖叫
雁斜斜飞　保持对人的警觉
而人　缝合一生那冗长的排比句

公园暗绿的一角
他的荒谬　是还渴望
坐进一把锈铁椅子的炎症

　　　　"河者，水之气……"

书上写了　梧桐叶
又黄又皱的手紧贴路面
又咸　又狂暴　空中脚蹼纷飞
蹬着看不见的水

　　　　　昨夜远在千里之外
一夜　冬天就挤满早晨
拼命甩着被枯枝穿成一串的死鱼
屋顶上　灰白的鳔膨胀
压迫树木幽暗　吻合一首诗的心情

他四十七岁　一道石阶也被自己磨光了

What Water Confirms

1

sure   wind is leaving along itself too
inherit   crystal ripples in surnames
autumn carries people who stroll   people who jog
and the iron bells hanging all over the November treetops
turn around a street corner   warm
                                        like elsewhere's autumn

all forms of the past lick towards a golden rim

sure   along his afternoon
the pitch-black asphalt road ponders this house
a bird's head rots to expose the skull

                        'and water flows westward again,
                        passes the big town, saying...'

written on the book   a fall of rain from deep breathing
the blue injected into apples   full of the shrill screams of schoolkids
wild geese in slanting flight   staying alert for humans
and a man   sews up the superfluous parallel lines of his life

a dark green corner in the park
his absurdity   or eagerness
sits into the inflammation of a rusting chair

                        'river, the breath of water...'

written on the book   leaves of Chinese plane trees
hands both sallow and wrinkled stick fast to the pavement
both salty   and violent   a random eddy of flippers in air
staring at the unseen water

                last night is beyond a thousand miles away
all night   winter is crammed with mornings
desperately flinging away dead fish skewered on withered twigs
on the roof   greyish white swim bladders swelling
pressing the trees dim   matching the mood of a poem

he is forty-seven   also a self-polished flight of smooth stone stairs

打着沉溺的拍子　花园支离破碎的肉
不知道时间除了在雨声中坍塌
不记得毁灭　除了在楼下
变成一只血淋淋的漏斗

体内推移的岸　暴露一刹那
就搁在厨房窗台上　肯定
窗外有个疯子佝偻着　有颗头哐哐冲撞
芦花四散　河一缕缕撕成絮状

他心里的盐认出了此地

indulgently beating time   fragments of flesh in a garden
unaware of time except for the collapse in the sound of rain
not remembering destruction   except for downstairs
changing into a bloody funnel

an elapsing shore in the body   exposes an instant
put it on the kitchen windowsill   sure
outside the window a madman is crooking his back   a head is banging against it
reed catkins disperse   river is torn into strands of cotton

the salt in his heart recognises this place

二

两部书一模一样　他重写
就走在另一个人梦里
欧洲的竹子一夜间全开花了
竹叶间的言辞　终于随风飘去
路口　翻开星期日烂牡蛎的天色
揉着鲜花市场上无数剪断的脖子

两部书相距千年　他穿行
于一个裹在羽毛里的季节
另一个自己中另一场梦呓
河水不停回顾
两把磨得雪亮的利刃交叉
溺死者吟哦的冷
编成兴高采烈的古籍

欧洲的竹子听到最初漂洋过海的那一根
牵着会爆炸的点
又决定迷路了

迷失在鲜花间　第五次看见
乌鸦啄烂枝头最后的苹果
这地点就不同了　这发黑的柄
叼在光年嘴里　星空溅出
拧断的一刹那　回忆录中摘抄的一刹那

丝织窗帘遮不住时
总被一个电视新闻的疆耗开始
街头　两个黑天使练习传球
一只圣诞铃铛踢进窗户
蜡烛爆炸　海鸥像受惊的侨民四散
一个关在飞机里的末日狭小而绝对
急转弯　撞上紧紧尾随的现实

到处都是借用的　死后溢出的香
到处　两只乳头温柔摩擦
一大捧玫瑰　一座红艳的绞盘
另一双手在梦的缺口中绞动云朵
在　他从未醒来而风拒绝吹去的方向

千　年
苹果慢得惊人地落到地上

58

2

two identical books   he rewrites
walk in someone else's dreams
the bamboos of Europe all bloom in one night
words between bamboo leaves   gone with the wind at last
street corners   spread out Sunday's rotting-oyster sky
kneading numberless beheaded necks in the flower market

two books a thousand years apart   he threads his way
through a season wrapped in feathers
another sleep talk in another self
river endlessly looking back
two sharp crisscross swords polished snow-bright
coldness chanted by the drowned
is compiled into an ecstatic classic

when the bamboos of Europe hear about the first ocean-going stem
pulling an explosive point
they decide they are lost again

lost among the flowers   see for the fifth time
crows peck and mash the last apple on the branch
this place will then be different   this blackening handle
dangle from the mouth of light years   the starlit sky spatter out
the moment of twisting and breaking   the moment of extraction from memoirs

when the silk blind can't conceal
always initiated by the worst possible news on TV
a street corner   two black angels practise passing a ball
a small Christmas bell is kicked in through the window
candles explode   seagulls scurry in all directions like frightened expats
a judgment day locked in an aeroplane is narrow and absolute
take a sharp turn   collide with the reality following close behind

everywhere is borrowed   fragrance spilling out after death
everywhere   two nipples gently rubbing
a big bunch of roses   a gaudy red capstan
another pair of hands twisting clouds at the gap of dreams
in   the direction where he never wakes up, where the wind refuses to blow

thousand   years
with terrifying slowness, apples fall to the ground

三　离题诗

墓园

这宁静渗透了水，水缓缓穿过那些身体
水缓缓带走那棵最后的白桦树
你们的墓碑，被风声、鸟儿和新的一年忘记

这宁静吸饱了阳光，像沼泽一样金黄
灌木触动那些嘴唇，那些小小的
似乎鲜红的果实，在傍晚吐露纯洁的秘密
那些手不知道，为什么当它们融解
旷野上就升起一条条从未聆听过足音的小路

现在你们脸上泛滥了野茅草的颜色
经过冬天，蟋蟀叫着
仍然梦想一座被篱笆环绕的小房子
那儿，只有一阵风、一只鸟和昨天盘旋过

现在，久久等待的那个黎明
降临到你们不变的黑暗上面
那听不见任何歌曲的耳朵，在地下张开
淡蓝的不起眼的小花，被一片落叶盖住
你们始终望着天空，不再怕暴风雨——

这宁静，这仍在一分一秒衰老的心
一座遗失了路标，悬挂于泥土黑夜中的村庄
一种没有人来也没有人去的永恒

没有悲哀，也没有云。风声和鸟儿
都焦急地跟着昨天飞走
你们什么也不知道，只有最后一刻的微笑
是水。是太阳。是寂静。

（一九八四年，为黑龙江知青墓地而作）

3 *An off-theme verse*
GRAVEYARD

this quiet has been soaked in water, water slowly penetrating these bodies
water slowly carrying away the last white birch
your tombstones forgotten by the sound of the wind, birds and the new year

this quiet has absorbed enough sunlight, as golden as the marshes
shrubs stir those lips, those tiny little
fruits that look bright red, confessing pure secrets at evening
those hands don't know why as they melt
field paths that have never listened to footsteps will appear one by one

now your faces are flooded with the colour of a meadow of wild grass
winter has passed, crickets are chirping
still dreaming of a little house inside a fence
there, only a gust of wind, a bird and yesterday have hovered in the air

now the dawn you've waited for so long
falls onto your unchanging darkness
the ears that can't hear any songs are spread out under ground
inconspicuous pale blue flowers are covered by a single fallen leaf
you look up at the sky all the while, no longer afraid of rainstorms –

this quiet, this heart which still ages with every minute, every second
a village with missing road signs, hanging suspended in the muddy night
an eternity where no one comes, no one goes

no sorrow, no clouds. The sound of wind and the birds
flutter anxiously away with yesterday
you know nothing at all, only that the final instant's smile
is water is the sun is silence.

[1984, written for the graveyard of the young urban intellectuals who were exiled
to Heilongjiang]

四

在哈克尼 河流是一位隐身的神
深秋涨水才看得见 街道下面
冰川在凹槽里继续磨着
木版《水经注》俯向漂泊的涵义
此日独一无二的在

沁着光
被一只水鸟的翻飞――穿透

乔治亚 维多利亚 爱德华 伊利沙白

          要是魏或者唐呢

一座黄铜壁炉间浮游死者的灰
一对象牙白的眼珠目送他的脚步
一串小公园的名字漾开
    嘴边一圈圈的绿

小教堂 船头总有一口钟拼命敲响
模仿黄浦江浓雾中那一次

地貌抱紧一个弃婴
破汽车抛在路边 距离
象只马达被挖走 要是
一行中文诗纵容雨把房间搬得更空呢

水 潜回一片沼泽的古老听力
水 也厌倦了流动吧

      错过 也累了
一堵红砖墙象道时间的平行线
夜夜延长 就有一个人孤独的结构
让他臆想那是他要的 舵
干裂于风中 珠光在牡蛎熟睡的体内抽打
哈克尼象首绝句 珍藏让他怕的月色
日历翻过去 本地口音的小广场
揣着肮脏的鸽子摔得粉碎

4

in Hackney   the river is a hidden god
only seen when the autumn floods rise   under the streets
glaciers keep grinding in the rebated trench
a woodblock *Waterways Classic Annotated* bows to the meaning of wandering
this day uniquely, once only, exists

soaked with light
pierced again and again by the fluttering of a water bird

Georgia   Victoria   Edward   Elizabeth

                    what if it was the Kingdom of Wei or the Tang Dynasty?

a brass fireplace where the ashes of the dead drift
a pair of ivory-white eyeballs gaze after his footsteps
a string of small parks' names spread like ripples
                    rings of green by the mouth

a chapel   a bell always desperately ringing at the prow
imitating the one on the Whampoa in heavy fog

landforms hold a foundling tight
wrecked cars abandoned at the roadside   distance
is dug away like a motor   what if
one line of Chinese poetry lets the rain empty a room even more

water   dives back to the ancient hearing of the marshes
water   probably weary of flowing too

                    missed it   tired too
a red brick wall is like a line running parallel to time
night after night extends   then there's the lonely structure of an individual
let him guess that's what he wants   rudder
dries up and cracks in the wind   pearly light thrashes in the sleeping oyster
Hackney is like a short Chinese verse   treasuring the moonlight she fears
leaves of a calendar turned over   a little plaza with a local accent
holds dirty pigeons to its bosom and breaks into pieces

Waterways Classic Annotated: A major work of geographical writing by Li Daoyuan
(*d.* 527). Its forty chapters trace the various river courses of China, providing a wealth
of anecdotal and historical material concerning cities and areas through which the rivers
pass.

五

"少禽多鬼......河水之所潜也"

他知道 这口罗马石棺是空的
浮雕在水上的名字耗尽了考古学
博物馆的玻璃柜子 那虚构的恒温
更象被挖出来的风景
　　她任我们抚摸 半裸的大理石
　　催促不懂激情的手
　　她任我们喝醉了潜入一道雪白的折痕
　　夕阳在未成废墟的墙外落下
　　棕榈涮洗一只摘掉的眼珠时
　　绿意 像孔雀进驻的蓝又冷又亮
　　这道情人守不住的边界
　　战士有什么用 我们在北风中崩溃
　　如壁画上一条纤细得
　　被颜色压垮的线
　　听她对胸前金黄的小蛇说
　　吻吧 帝国死在身后
　　无非一个取悦的形象

"乌托之西，有悬渡之国"

他的小丘上 这眼快干枯的泉水
俯瞰着史诗 这条黑狗
选中一株垂柳去撒尿
　　她在我们冻裂的膝盖间走动
　　我们五指脱落 已无力
　　把矛扎透腹腔直到尾骨 或把河道掘得更深
　　　　像想当王的人说的
　　船队焚烧时 只有她回到梦里
　　萨克森白雪下片片绿草
　　我们穿过田野 一路想着她的性
　　有点儿臭的温暖东西
　　猪卧入火塘的灰 她站起来
　　裙子响着象叮嘱下一次
　　　　　　可谁认识这个冬天啊
　　谁的嗓音正沿着灌木的刺细细升起
　　牙根被沼泽涂满棕红色
　　我们挣着铁丝穿住的锁骨
　　大喊 又被弹回
　　她一转身时间就消失

5

'with fewer animals and more ghosts... where rivers hide'

he knows   this Roman sarcophagus is empty
names carved in water exhaust archaeology
glass cabinets in museums   that fictional constant temperature
even more like excavated scenery
    she lets us caress   half-naked marble
    urgent hands that know nothing of passion
    she lets us get drunk and dive into a snow-white fold
    the sun sets beyond a wall not yet ruined
    when palm trees brush a plucked-out eyeball
    the feel of green   cold and bright like the blue where peacocks are stationed
    this border that lovers can't guard
    what's the use of soldiers   we're collapsing in the northerly wind
    like a line on a fresco so fine
    it falls under the pressure of colour
    listen to what she tells the small golden snake in her bosom
    kiss it   a kingdom dies behind the body
    nothing but a pleasing image

'in the west of Utopia lies the kingdom of Hanging Ferry'

on his mound   this soon to dry up spring
looks down at an epic   this black dog
picks a weeping willow to piss on
she walks between our chapped kneecaps
our fingers all fall off   exhausted already
stab a spear through the belly to the tailbone   or dig the river deeper
              like those who would be king say
when the fleet burns   she's the only one returning to a dream
green laws lie under white Saxon snow
we pass through fields   thinking about her gender on the way
a warm thing that stinks a bit
a pig that lies in the ashes of a fiery pool   she stands up
her skirt making noises as if it warns of next time
              but who recognises this winter
whose thready voice is rising along the thorny shrubs
hums painted reddish brown by the marshes
we try to get free from the wires that thread through our collarbones
cry out   be bounced back again
once she turns around, time vanishes

"天下之多者水也"

他无须地图也找到了

这块野餐的花毯子

天鹅腋窝下　河谷无须阴暗的目录

远方打开包装纸　矫正

一只蘑菇的视线

　　她说　周年的日子　并不

　　大于平面复印的其他日子

　　颐和园里一艘石船驶入荷花们的肉色

　　放逐　就捏碎一枚怀旧的蕊

　　我们这只瓶子盛着给自己的信

　　总在追赶一页大海的原稿

　　她说　生命把人涂掉　而书写

　　虚幻地留住

　　　　　　　唯一停下的瞬间

　　　　　　　是当你爱过

　　只一会儿　舌头被母语荡着

　　鬼魂拈出米粒大的昔日

　　一晃　河水奔逃象去摸那道闪电

　　候鸟跟着飞　水花四溅低低起跑

　　一本书接一本书丢进宇宙

她被挖出时笑得更欢

　　毒牙的珠串还佩在胸前

'what the world abounds in, is water'

with no need for a map he has found
this flowery picnic blanket for
under the armpits of a swan   a valley needs no gloomy catalogue
in a distant place brown paper is opened out   rectifying
a mushroom's line of sight
   she says   anniversary   is not
bigger than other duplicated dates
in the Summer Palace a stone boat sails into the flesh-coloured lotuses
exile   crumbles with fingers a pistil yearning for the past
this bottle of ours that holds a letter to ourselves
always chases a page of the ocean's manuscript
she says   life erases humans   and writing
persists under an illusion
                  the only instant that stops
             is when you've loved
  for only a short while   your tongue is rocked by your mother tongue
ghosts pick out the grain-sized past
  in a flash   the river dashes like it's trying to touch that bolt of lightning
migratory birds fly along   their low-level start splashing water in all directions
  book after book is thrown into space

when she is dug out she laughs more happily
  still in her bosom, a string of venomous fangs

六　离题诗

又十年了，哈德逊河

而后　我们背对象征

坐进　另一条河上
深蓝色房间的深蓝色角落

听觉更黑时　栈桥依着水低语过十年
小公园里　树木嫩绿的手风琴拉响了十年
孩子们冲下从四月到四月的台阶

云冲下一个倒影　水面一明一暗
松鼠被压烂的内脏就翻开
血红的照相册　隔着玻璃蜇人的现实
手浸湿也摸不到列队的日子

河　悬在过去窗口的空白教科书
提问着现在仍仅仅一页　流浪不用学
厌倦　栓着一只水鸟低飞
回游的漩涡　给全世界的高楼一个出口
逃　逃向塑料花　消失不用学

哈德逊酷似一个风声组成的名字
灯火斜眼走过　酷似藏在人体内的鬼火
被拧亮　酷似想吹灭就吹灭时
黄昏录制在天边的瑰丽的缺口
谁读懂了　就住进一首诗
发生不完的往事

房间中的房间　灌满十年的水
角落在角落里　漆着远方的深蓝色
我们坐着的姿势永远背对大海
听浪碎了　瓦砾狠狠砸着十年
电话线断了　呼救声盲目飘了十年
河流忘却的颜色　忘不了
每天　高空中一捧红艳的钢铁垂直崩落

焚烧不用学　一把灰固定在
闭紧的眼睛里　月亮像只被摘除的核
用女低音唱着　每条河谷的安魂曲
每个漂走的地点死一次才显形一次

68

6 *An off-theme verse*
ANOTHER DECADE, HUDSON RIVER

then   we turn our backs to the symbols

sit into   another river
a dark blue corner of a dark blue room

when hearing is blacker   ten years the jetty has leaned whispering against water
in the little park   ten years the tender green accordion of trees has played
children charging down the April to April steps

clouds charging down their reflection   water now bright now dark
and squirrel's pulped organs open
a blood-red photo album   reality stings even through glass
even a soaked hand couldn't touch the lined-up days

river   a blank textbook hanging from the past window
questioning now only the single remaining page   no need to learn vagrancy
weariness   tethered to a water bird flying low
the spinning whirlpool   exit for all the world's skyscrapers
flee   flee to plastic flowers   no need to learn vanishing

Hudson just like a name formed by the sound of the wind
lamplight's passing glance   just like ghost fire hidden in human bodies
switched on   just like a notch blown away at will
a rosy notch twilight recorded on the sky
whoever has understood it   will live into a poem
unending past events

room in a room   filled with water of a decade
corner in a corner   painting the dark blue of distance
the way we sit forever turning our backs on the ocean
listening to the waves shatter   rubble savagely smashing a decade
telephone lines broken   cries for help blindly float through a decade
river the colour of forgetting   can't forget
each day   two hands full of crimson steel tumbling straight down

no need to learn burning   handful of ash fixed in
tight-shut eyes   moon like a scooped-out pip
singing contralto   requiem for every river valley
every place that flows away appears each time after dying

岸铺在脚下　已被抽掉过上千次
一根惨白的鱼骨总有闪着磷光的另一端
只要忍受　拍打一生的
诀别　再推出今夜

用一个房间被扔进宇宙的样子
测量这艘沉船还能下沉多少
我们背对画成地平线的零
还得迁徙多远　疯狂的蓝才足够黑
丢了的口音里　哈德逊紧挨着
一只埋在中国古老村口的青石井圈
毁灭摸到自己仅有一天的直径
一滴　饱含留给我们的冰雪
那幸存的美丽和幸存的冷酷

banks paved underfoot   have been thousands of times removed
a pale fishbone always has another end glowing with phosphorescent light
endurance   to slap a lifetime's final
farewell   pushing out tonight again

with the look of a room thrust into the universe
survey how much this sunken ship could further sink
our backs turned to zero drawn as the horizon
how much farther it migrates   then crazy blue is blue enough to be black
in a lost accent   Hudson pressed against
a bluestone wellhead buried at the gate of an ancient Chinese village
destruction touches its own diameter of one day
one drop   gathers snow left for us
with the beauty of survivors and the cruelty of survivors

七 离题诗

信

"……平静的乐趣"（父亲的信）

水做的窗户关上一扇时也打开一扇
水是一封信　总投向更远处
你的手还伸过黑暗轻拍儿子的睡眠
血缘的方言低语　夜最耐读
八十年　灯蛾翩翩

一场雨　构思这家书
老花镜和摘下的目光　搁在桌上
茶杯　向一刹那前的玻璃回顾
那儿祖父咆哮　男孩儿朝背叛的床
再挪一寸　革命涨满童声的大红大绿

那儿　一只青花梅瓶被内蕴的猖狂
所压碎　爸爸　你人生的诗韵
还拎着儿子的听觉　贴紧十一岁的墙
他们逼出一个不像你的声音
弱　却是否认的　置身于红袖章

的事外　文竹枝叶葱翠　在否认
词的内脏中有个空白横扫的世纪
得弱成残月或陌生人　未来才像体温
涌进这笔尖　你挂号寄出你自己
收信者越近

写　越象一场璀灿的退席
幽暗啊　蓄满一只幽独的眼角
儿子的血就蘸着你微笑的那一滴
回信　瞄准世界起跑的那条
横格线　你给的心跳会应和你

你给的舌尖　舔　就取消
母亲死的咸味　死　堆垒生的一半
爸　这遂道没有导游　你最棒的逍遥
是粘紧信封　让嗓音静谧如蚕
织一夜丝光闪闪的茧子——"一切　安好"

72

7 *An off-theme verse*
LETTER

'...the joy of tranquillity' (father's letter)

water-made windows, one closed as the other opens
water is a letter   always thrown farther away
your hand even stretches across the dark to pat your son's slumber
blood-kin dialect whispers   night takes the longest time to be read
eighty years   fluttering moths

          a fall of rain   composes this note from home
long-sighted glasses and vision taken off   put down on a table
teacup   looks back at the glass of a moment ago
there grandfather roars   a boy faces a betraying bed
move one more inch   revolution swollen with the bright red-green of kid's voices

there   a blue and white *meiping* vase, by the wildness it contains
is crushed   dad   the rhymes of your life
still carry your son's hearing   stuck close to an eleven-year-old wall
they force out a voice unlike yours
weak   but denying   aloof from the red-armband

affair   yellow-green asparagus ferns   denying
in the guts of words lies a century swept over by blankness
to be weak as crescent moon or stranger   future to be like body
temperature
surging into the tip of this pen   you send yourself by registered mail
the closer the recipient

          writing   the more like a blinding leaving of the banquet
oh, gloom   fills a quiet corner of the eye
your son's blood dipping in that smiling drop of yours
letter in reply   aims at the grid tape where
the world starts running   the heartbeat you give will be in tune with you

the tongue tip you give   licks   then cancels
the salty taste of mother's death   deaths   pile up into half a mortal life
dad   there's no guide in this tunnel   your greatest transcendent bliss
is to seal tight an envelope   let the voices be stilled like a silkworm
knitting all night its silky cocoon – 'all's   well'

八

　　　　　他说
这不是地理书　而是记忆之书
这只白瓷浴缸里的水声
被远山中一弯河谷记着
千年之冷　自最上游
一口溶洞寻来
水下那个肉体　细看
是只血红的青蛙
皮撕掉　卵拥着一块玉

　　　　　他踩在青苔上说
这张床逆着早晨漂
每个被再次分娩的孩子
向回爬过甬道　温习一丛水草
拚贴在墙上的色情的风景

　　　　　他边沿着自己离去边说
谁向前　读河这本小小厚厚的书
谁就向后　读到自己的陌生
去拧干海底城市的灯火
去河边露宿　望月　垂钓
去体内一汪百分之七十的溶液里搁浅
竹子开花了
根　全力以赴繁殖一声惨叫

74

8

                                    he says
this is not a book on geography   but a book of memory
the sound of water in this white porcelain bathtub
is remembered by a river valley in distant hills
cold of a thousand years   comes from the uppermost reaches
a water-eroded cave finds
that underwater flesh   look closer
it's a blood-red frog
flayed   eggs embracing a piece of jade

                              he steps on the moss and says
this bed drifts against the morning
each child being reborn
crawls back to pass a corridor   revises a patch of waterweed
pornographic landscapes collaged on the wall

                              while leaving along himself he says
whoever goes forward   to read the river this tiny thick book
will go backward   to read up to his own unfamiliarity
to wring out the lamplight in submarine cities
to sleep on the riverbank   full moon   angling
to run aground in a pool of 70% solution of flesh and blood
bamboos have blossomed
root   going all out to reproduce a shriek of terror

九

"而不能辨其所在"
　　的是一场梦
他的小鳗鱼出没于洞穴
她有个分辨不出的母亲的嗓音
最后送来的箱子　轻得
弄伤了手　象不再假笑的时间
锈成一团暗绿的站台上
软软躺着具尸首
他完成的部份鲜美如花
一个纯视觉　却不知被谁看着
她的癌悄悄拧亮　被谁领着
来找谁　转告脱身的消息
　　　　死是梦中梦
睡了　才打开别的知识
他觉得一张木椅子的硬
来自透明的内部　尸首淡出
　　　　而谁摇着一杯溶液
她松手就忘了所有前世
他的稀薄在追问　这空出之处
腐蚀之处　水算不算一种留下的痕迹
当风吹来　梦交织　闹钟的爆炸
等于沉默

9

'can't identify its whereabouts'
it's a dream
his little baby eels haunt the cave
she has mother's voice, unrecognisable,
the last box delivered here   too light
has hurt hands   like time that no longer pretends to smile
on the platform rusted into a lump of dark green
a corpse softly reclines
his finished part bright and beautiful as the flowers
pure sense of sight   doesn't know it's looked at by someone
her cancer quietly twists to shine   led by someone
it's come to find someone   to pass on the news of escape
                                death is a dream in a dream
once asleep   then open up other knowledge
he thinks the hardness of a wooden chair
comes from its transparent interior   the corpse fades
                                and who's shaking a glass of solution
she loosens her grip and has forgotten all her past lives
his dilution is interrogating   this emptied place
this corroded place   can water be counted as a kind of left over trace
when the wind blows in   dreams intertwine   explosion of an alarm clock
equals silence

十　离题诗

慢板之一：莱比锡，秋天

在你动作里有一种慢　比树叶

亮出掌心的黄　还要慢

却一把抓住了音乐

慢板旅馆在莱比锡

秋天睡过莱比锡

战火　冷凝成街道上的问候

小学生口含一支进行曲

尿湿了雕像的空基座

他舌尖触到陌生的石头

琴键按下　空间发明了事物们的远眺

醒来就象谎言

只不过鸟唱着说

天花板用雪白的石膏繁衍一只豹子

扑向窗外蓝蓝的裸体

他嘴里　啤酒味粘粘拼贴着昨夜

一大股溢出冰箱的精液　偷听到子宫的温度

在你动作里有　风

推着嵌进琴声的行星慢慢转身

没有噩耗足够突然

打开浴缸和花园一道角门

死鱼的视野　追逐苹果烂到果核里

打开一万块桌布上的早餐

星期日　哪只器官不是喧嚣的乐池

天空犹豫不决地作曲

金鹧鸪从十一层阳台上俯瞰

他的云　低垂游客头顶一朵雕花

他的咳嗽声　在栏杆另一侧开凿旅途

一只右耳间隔情人们的亲吻

慢慢跃下

路口红灯更晚一拍

不信溅出的血是真的

（写到莱比锡　血就满地溅出）

你的动作延伸某一此刻　比秋天更长

树叶冶炼着簧片上的暗语　更有力

推他　用谎言醒两次

不信　听到的一切

10 *An off-theme verse*
ADAGIO ONE: LEIPZIG, AUTUMN

your movement has a kind of slowness   compared to leaves
yellow shining out from leaves' palms   it's even slower
                            but it catches the music in one grip
        Hotel Adagio in Leipzig
        autumn sleeps past Leipzig
        flames of war   condense into greetings on the street
                            school kids with a marching song in their mouths
                            piss on the empty sculpture pedestal
        his tongue tip touches an unfamiliar stone
piano keys are pressed   space has invented objects' distant gaze
        waking up is like a lie
                            only birds say in song
    ceiling uses snow-white plaster to multiply a leopard
    leaping to the blue nude outside the window
    in his mouth   sticky taste of beer is making a collage of last night
    semen hugely spilling from the fridge   overhears a womb's temperature
your movement has   the wind
turn slowly as it pushes planets embedded in music
                            no shocking news is sudden enough
    open the corner door between bathtub and garden
        dead fish's sight   chases an apple rotten to its core
        open out breakfasts on ten thousand tablecloths
                    Sunday   which organ isn't a noisy pond of happiness
sky hesitantly writes music
a golden partridge looks down from the eleventh floor balcony
        his clouds   hang low over the carved flower on a tourist's head
        his coughs   start on a journey beyond the railings
        a right ear separates lovers' kisses
jump slowly down
                    a red light at street corner one more beat later
                    disbelieve spilled blood is real
    (when Leipzig is written about   blood spilled from all over the ground)
your movement extends to one of these moments   longer than autumn
leaves are smelting the code words on reeds   stronger
    push him   wake up twice with lies
                    disbelieve   all that's been heard

十一　离题诗

慢板之二: 本地墓园, 夏天

                耳鸣持续
暴雨　今晚音乐会的序曲
　　一只和你一样大的蝉　带着你
　　哨音催促闷热的肉出土
　　松鼠像一个被电殛了的六月跳上墓碑
另一座图书馆塞满我
大理石的弱　在树根上东倒西歪
　　　　　右耳像语言
　　　　　被自己的回声压垮
　　世界在右边嘈杂一倍
　　只有你听见　小号似的器官关不上
　　只有右眼读到　扇着半张脸的绿
　　　　　　和律师手里的遗书一样黑
弱之膨胀先于所有崩溃
石灰质的呼喊　呕吐天鹅的断脖子
雷抛在河谷中　已来不及编辑
　　　　　　谁用许多嘴抢着说
　　树木放你走过时　摔着一件件紫水晶
　　玫瑰肥厚的舌苔上爆破声摔不碎
　　鸟儿烂掉一半
　　另一半大汗淋漓
　　　　　　乐队鬼魅得像光线
所有标明记忆的数字被一付摔断腿的眼镜架
加上　　负号
　　　　空也竞争着
成千对小铁块为演奏开始拼命鼓掌
我无穷无尽注视谢幕之时
　　是一场暴风雨从未打出这轮耳廓
　　或扎进你体内的蝉鸣如此绝对
　　　擦亮　坠
　　　　　落　今晚不是平衡的
　　死在夏天　孱弱的正是灿烂的
　　右前方淤满的听觉里一个逼近的聋
占据我　一刹那瞥见
　　脚下一只珍珠贝　如你一样毁掉自己
　　　　听到　不信的一切

                    80

11 *An off-theme verse*
ADAGIO TWO: LOCAL GRAVEYARD, SUMMER

tinnitus persists

rainstorm   overture to the concert tonight
    a cicada as big as you   is carrying you
    sound of a whistle urges sweltering flesh to come out of earth
    squirrels jump on gravestones like June electrocuted
another library is stuffed with me
weakness of marble   shown all around on recumbent roots
           the right ear is like language
           falling under the pressure of its own echoes
  the world is twice as noisy on the right
  only you hear   the trumpet-like human organ can't be shut down
  only the right eye reads   the green fanning half its face
           as black as the suicide note in a lawyer's hand
inflation of weakness precedes any collapse
calcareous shouting   vomits broken swan necks
snow thrown into river valleys   too late for editing
           who uses mouths to say in a rush
    when trees let you pass   pieces of purple crystal are cast one by one
    sounds of blasting can't break on the thick fur of roses' tongues
    one half of a bird rots
    another half drips with sweat
           the orchestra is ghostly as light
all numbers marking memories, by a broken-sided spectacle frame
are added with   a minus sign
           the void is competing too
a thousand pairs of tiny iron pieces applaud with all their might to start the show
when I endlessly gaze at the curtain call
    is it a rainstorm that never blows out of this ear
    or definite as the chirps of cicadas that garrison your body
      brush bright   fall
             down   tonight is off balance
    die in summer   the weak is exactly the dazzling
    deafness drawing near silted-up hearing on the right
occupies me   catch sight in an instant of
    an oyster shell under the feet   destroying itself like you do
           hear   all that's been disbelieved

十二　离题诗

慢板之三：火车上，春天

慢慢重温死后的蜜月
慢慢　看阳光从一具躯体中跳车
他用花苞努出小嘴
　　一间移动的候诊室　风景在点名
　　新绿漫不经心解开一件内衣
　　　　灌木调整天线
　　　　　　倒退着放映旧胶片
　　等待配音的春天里　我
　　　　反复穿过　像只坏了的助听器
慢　情敌们倒挂在篱笆上
　　女孩阴户夺目　一把把
　　　　　　手术刀迎面扑来
　　车窗钉牢飞鸟　剪票员
　　　　解剖无数往事
　　天空摇荡水杯　铁轨的针管
　　　　　　一场病又一场病把我抽回
　　　　　　到昨天　死者饮着艳遇
花朵们飞向断茎支撑的史前
星空　金黄的时刻表允许他尽情晚点
一直向南开　甩掉自己的影子
　　　　　　　夹进书里的铁玫瑰甩着远山
　　一朵池塘中的云　越白越像内脏
　　一场性交后满屋消毒的丁香
　　窗口反光中坐着护士
　　微微转身　从纯金的倒钩上摘掉现实
　　　　　　我不想听　因此聋了
他听了又听　世界是一件旧家俱
摆在死后退还的爱情里
　　　　没有肉体的爱
　　　　卷起距离的草图
　　远方分泌我　一串小爆炸
　　　　又亮又甜地
　　　　舔到焦点上
（接近莱比锡　想起蜜月有个题目）
死者慢得完美　那尽可能的温柔
　　被跳车的人带在身上
　　　　　信　听不到的一切

82

12 *An off-theme verse*

slowly revive a honeymoon after death
slowly   watch sunlight jump off the body's train
he pouts his little lips with flower buds
    a moving hospital waiting-room   scenery is taking a roll call
    fresh green casually unbuttons an undergarment
        shrubs adjust an aerial
                projecting old films in reverse
    in spring that waits to be dubbed   I
        pass through repeatedly   like a broken-down
hearing aid
slow   rivals in love hang upside down on the fence
    a girl's vulva dazzles the eye   one by one
        scalpels throw themselves onto my face
    birds are nailed to train windows   a conductor
        dissects countless past events
    sky is rocking a glass   syringes of the rails
        one sickness after another draws me back
        to yesterday   the dead are drinking brief encounters
flowers fly to prehistory supported by broken stems
starlit sky   a golden timetable lets him be as late as he wants
head straight south   cast off its own shadow
        iron roses pressed between pages pull away from distant hills
    a cloud in the pond   the whiter it is the more it looks like guts
    a roomful of sterilised post-coital lilacs
    a nurse sitting in light reflected by the window
    turns slightly round   plucks reality off a solid gold barb
        I don't want to listen   and so I turn deaf
he listens again and again   the world is a piece of old furniture
placed in love returned after death
        love without flesh
        rolls up a draft of distance
    a distant place secretes me   a series of small explosions
    brightly and sweetly
        lick onto the focal point
    (approaching Leipzig   recall that a honeymoon has a topic)
the dead are so slow they attain perfection   that best possible gentleness
    is carried by the one who jumps off the train
        believe   all that can't be heard

十三

云像一万个尿频的女人急急奔跑
而官方的蓝　无动于衷地看着
雪猛下一阵　鸽子们日常的演奏课
坠毁到屋脊那根弦后面
一大把郁金香嚣张的红
和无味　袭击鼻孔
　　　　　哈克尼无非一组意象

渗漏得比一个地址更深
一棵梨树就给街角一面狂想的白旗
一次暂停　沿着假设的茎攀援
充斥他到期的四十七岁
向生活投降无非接受一场手术

　　　　　模拟一只精心结构
　　　　　自己形状和颜色的海星

把旅程布置进一个脚下的死扣里面去
把移动　分行处决
云再变　天空收养一群蝎子
　　　　响应疼的必要性

他一生遭遇的人像这地点躲不开
他远远回避的自我　越修改越来到
哈克尼　慢慢显形为一个性格时
一场瓦解选中回家的他
与融雪中一枝干透的迎春齐步
　　　　回到眼帘后边
　　　　细细玩味被耗尽的快感

clouds are like ten thousand women hurrying in frequent urination
the official blue   looks at them unmoved
a sudden snowfall   pigeons' daily classes on instrumental performance
crash behind that string on the roof ridge
a big bunch of tulips arrogant red
and scentless   assail the nostrils
                        Hackney is simply a group of images

seeping more deeply than an address
a pear tree then gives the street corner a white flag of pipe dreams
a pause   climbs along the presumed stem
flooding his expired forty-seven years of age
to surrender to living is simply to be operated on

                    imitate a starfish that meticulously constructs
                    its own shape and colour

arrange an itinerary into a tight knot under the feet
separately execute   movements
clouds change again   sky adopts a swarm of scorpions
                    echoing the necessity of pain

people he meets all his life are as unavoidable as this place
the self he avoids from afar   the more amended the more likely it comes to
Hackney   when it slowly appears as a disposition
Complete collapse picks him up on his way home
to synchronise with a dry branch of winter jasmine in melted snow
                    return behind the iris of the eye
                    delicately ponder the delight of being exhausted

十四

阿尔嫩如婴儿
他的河都在　这道肉做的河床中
易　津沱　哈德逊　帕拉玛塔　被加宽
直到李　细细窄窄而无限
奢望着呼吸的结尾

　　　这反光发育一个无过程
　　　这部书从未让一滴水流失

坐在桌前就听见波浪
给他的岸　更换湿湿的名字
给盲文　分配一根棕黄滑腻的食指

摸了又摸　早晨的仪式
一杯绿茶形而上的赤裸
一支端茶的手　穿过人生虚设的靶心
一口饮下遍地断头鲜花的绝对

忍受　更亮更难忍的
发育一根唱针的阳光

　　　时间的秘密是这个空间
　　　诗守着肉体再添一点儿重
　　　对称的美学　对称于皮肤下溃散的
　　　一微秒

就色情地否认了来历
纸上的河底　把日子掏得更空
让他构思在一个转弯被甩掉的
猝然点燃一丛桃花耀眼撩人的
蓝白相间的蕊血肉跳跃

　　　唯一的激情是混淆前世与来世

当小水鸟唧唧一叫暴露出裂缝

14

the Aare is young like a baby
her riverside city all   in this flesh-made riverbed
change   Hutuo   Hudson   Parramatta   broadened
up to Lea   thin, narrow and infinite
wildly wish an end to breathing

          this reflection of light develops a zero process
          this book has never lost a drop of water

sit in front of the desk and hear the waves
help his shore   change into a dripping name
allocate to Braille   a smooth brownish-yellow forefinger

touch again and again   morning ceremonies
metaphysically naked in a cup of green tea
a hand holding the tea   passes through the nominal bull's-eye of life
drink in one gulp the absoluteness of beheaded flowers everywhere

endure   the brighter, more unendurable
sunlight that develops into a stylus

          time's secret is this space
          poetry guarding human bodies gains more weight
        symmetrical aesthetics   symmetrical to that one tiny second
        which disperses in defeat under the skin

pornographically deny the source and origin
river bottom on paper   hollows out the days even more
let him design what is thrown off on the bends
suddenly kindle what dazzles in a grove of peach blossom

alternate blue and white stamens of flesh and blood leaping

        the only passion is for mixing up past lives and future ones

as small water birds chirp to expose the cracks

十五 离题诗

完成

————赠 R.B.

诗的饱满追随一只死猫泡胀的躯体
经过我们窗下 洪水的匀速
使放着酒杯的小桌逆流行驶
向哪儿 这座停电的城市

早许诺了灌满狂风的黑
让公园里排练一场互相目送
颠簸的座位上两条白鳗在朗诵
四脚僵直的月光鼠只剩好听的名字

闭紧双眼才飞到满月那么高
十八层楼上一枚空的图章打进肉里
斟着 今夜将一口口喝醉的
数 第几块广告牌正从铆钉枝头起跳

拧断的微笑 翻滚 溶解在海上
我们不知第几个海的第几个
命运 一幅泼墨 收回一生磷光的足迹
悬挂于两堵相隔万里的墙上

15 *An off-theme verse*
COMPLETION
for R.B.

plumpness of poetry pursues a dead cat's puffed-up body
passes beneath our windows   the steady speed of flood water
drives a small table holding a wine glass against the current
to where   this blacked-out city

long ago promised the gale-filled dark
let the scene of gazing after each other be rehearsed in the park
two white eels reciting on bumpy seats
only the sweet name of moonlit mice with rigor mortis is left

eyes tight shut to fly as high as the full moon
on the eighteenth floor an empty seal stamps into flesh
pouring   what will be gulped down tonight until intoxication
count   which number billboard is taking off from the rivets' tips

twisted and broken smiles   rolling   dissolve on the sea
we don't know which number sea is in which sequence
destiny   splashed-ink painting   withdraws a life's phosphorescent footprints
hangs on two walls ten thousand miles apart

十六　离题诗

湖

——————赠 D.M.

井也死了　我坠落到井底的目光
更破碎时就变成了你的
或湖的　盯着五彩的石子向下倾斜
暗金色树林象个潜泳学校

再跳一次　向倒影中再摸一次
亮着聋着的一片水
张开第三只肺　一根蓝黑的翎毛飘落
低于人　如果终极的崩溃存在

谁把月亮放到小小阳台的正对面
谁的夜　慢慢垮进自己的语言
盐味还在唇上　舌尖已舔着
风的口音　我从一个鸟窝里掏出过

而你轻轻把蛋壳敲破
找到那孩子　还向下探望呢
还以为真有一个世界等着被打捞
像傻笑背后有假牙　牙缝间
　　　　　　进退不得的是母语

16 An off-theme verse
LAKE

for D.M.

the well died too   when my gaze had fallen to the bottom of the well
more broken up, it turned into your
or the lake's   staring at the colourful cobbles tilting down
dark golden grove like a diving school

jump once more   touch once more into the inverted reflection
a sheet of deaf shining water
expand the third lung   a blackish blue plume drifting down
below the human   if an ultimate collapse exists

who puts the moon just opposite a tiny little balcony
whose night   slowly strides into his own language
salty taste still on the lips   tongue tip has been licking
the wind's accent   I was taken from a nest

and you gently broke the eggshell open
to find the child   even looked down inside
even thought there really was a world waiting to be salvaged
like the dentures behind the smirk   between teeth
                    mother tongue is caught in a dilemma

十七 离题诗

玫瑰
————赠友友

要找我们那一瓣 得等到冬天 傍晚
落日把对岸几扇窗子提炼成黄金
又灭了 回家的古老话题
噎死于自身的恐惧

要问 水下多远 泛起那嫣红
暮色蹒跚多远亲着一枚耳垂
天鹅低飞 翅尖触及水面另一对翅尖
血淋淋倒映的腋窝

指出我们的梦 不可能更远
地平线总有你在一张床上的样子
甜得象假设 我得修饰我的嗅觉
一个岛像一滴油亮晶晶浮着

回 是否就让肉里渗出一抹灰
卷着边缘像在说 一生太慢了
花瓣被毁掉 只需要冷透的一刹那
黑透 静静合进夜空那重重叠叠的一朵

17 *An off-theme verse*
ROSE

for Yoyo

to find that petal of ours   we must wait for winter   evening
the setting sun refines the windows on the other shore into gold
extinguished again   the age-old topic of going home
choked to death by terror of itself

we have to ask   how far beneath the water   that bright red is suffused
how far does twilight limp to kiss an earlobe
swans fly low   wing tips touch wing tips on the water's surface
blood-dripping inverted reflection of armpits

point out that our dreams   can't be farther away
the horizon always has the look of you on a bed
sweet as an assumption   I have to adorn my sense of smell
an island is like a glittering floating drop of oil

return   whether or not to let a smear of ash seep from the flesh
rolling up the edges as if to say   all of a life is too slow
the petal is destroyed   needing only a really cooled-down moment
really black   quietly integrated into the overlapping flowers of the night sky

十八 离题诗

洪荒时代
————赠张枣

空旷的水银色连成一片　侵蚀到眼里
湖畔青苔累累的木桌上摆着
我们的孤独　押着雪的韵脚
一万张鸟嘴重复一种白

时间平铺直叙　像野餐结束不了
我们坐着　也指爪碧绿
抠入死寂就成为死寂明月的一部分
写得好　就写至阴暗生命的报复

有鹤的家风　就出一张鱼的牌吧
水原地转身捻着石质的小骨头
不转　一半倒进湖中的大树同时有四季
蜗牛被发霉的听觉牵着爬　爬

星空的小港有道木头跳板
船却烂了　帆紧紧卷起象从未发明过
我们形同受苦　被再发明一次
甩掉人类　关进自己的光尽情兴高采烈

18 *An off-theme verse*

CHAOTIC ERA

for Zhang Zao

quicksilver hue merges into a vast expanse   corrodes into the eyes
the moss-covered wooden table at the lakeside displays
our loneliness   detaining end rhymes of snow
ten thousand beaks repeat one kind of white

the factual description of time   endless as a picnic
we're sitting   fingers and claws dark green too
digging into deathly silence to be part of the deathly silent moon
write well   then write up to the revenge of gloomy life

a family tradition of having cranes   so show a fish card
water turns around at the same spot, twisting a small stony bone in its fingers
no turning   a big tree half fallen into the lake has four simultaneous seasons
snails are led to crawl by mouldy hearing   crawl

the little harbour of the starry sky has a wooden springboard
yet a ship was wrecked   tightly rolled-up sail looks as not yet invented
our apparent suffering   to be re-invented
to get rid of humans   lock into one's own light and be utterly jubilant

十九

要是早春也在注释否定的美学呢
雨和雪　交替的仪式
沿着她湿漉漉的曲线

异乡不是一个考题
体温才是　掠过窗前的鸟不是一声抽泣
激情才是

一朵小小的苹果花
像个女妖袅袅升上去年洗净的枝头
要是乌鸦又在刺探自己的饥饿
要是刺探一种死　而想不碰皮肤
只抚摸低低悬在那儿的月光呢

哈克尼有个岛的轮廓

在他心里　否定大海的移动
在她身上　否定意义能消失

19

what if early spring is annotating negative aesthetics too
rain and snow   alternate rituals
along her dripping wet shape

a foreign land isn't an exam question
but body temperature is   a bird that sweeps past windows isn't a sob
but passion is

a tiny little apple blossom
curls upward like a sorceress to the branch tip cleaned last year
what if a crow is spying on its own hunger again
what if one spies on a kind of death   but wants not to touch skin
only to caress the moonlight hanging down low

Hackney has the shape of an island

in his heart   deny the move of ocean
on her body   deny that meanings can vanish

二十

"河之为言荷也"

"随地下处而遇流也"

关于那些他　他能记得什么
关于水的书　再读还是沉溺
双向流来的河直逼一个人的空白

水声雕塑桌上一株虎皮兰
水声　追着一朵云扫描
骸骨们仍死死坚持发绿的性质
春天重复过多少次
草根铐在抽搐上　铐着讴歌
他的屈从　被誊为中年之美

竹杖点点　海鸥一片片灰羽毛被风掀着
脚步慢下来　日子暗暗加速
到这个湍急的什么也不写的下午
眼眶边　一块白石窗台像条地平线
远远被卷走

星际间　水的孤独
像无数光年狠狠砸入一只人类的子宫

虎皮兰用金色条纹怀抱的那只
他杜撰出整个河谷去冲洗的那只
岛的尽头　满月还为激情空着

春夜杜撰出淡淡的甜
瞎子们　杜撰城市四面八方的灯火
捣毁于一盏永久失忆的烛火
点燃就是紫丁香　像艘拖轮拖着
不在的地理学

在　之前和之后两个上游
放肆夹紧的死角里

20

'*river*, like *lotus*, is pronounced *ho*'

'it flows through places under the ground'

about those hims   what can he remember
the book about water   read it again and still sink
bi-directional river presses up to a person's blankness

sound of water carves a tiger lily on the table
sound of water   is chasing a cloud to scan it
skeletons still rigidly insist on the nature of turning green
how many times spring has been repeated
grass roots handcuff twitches   eulogising in handcuffs
his submission   praised as the beauty of middle age

the brief touch of a bamboo cane   seagulls' grey feathers lifted by the wind
footsteps slow down   days secretly speed up
to this rapidly flowing afternoon when nothing is written
at the eye sockets   a white stone windowsill like the horizon
is being swept far far away

interstellar   loneliness of water
fiercely smashes into a human womb like numberless light years

the bit that a tiger lily embraces with golden stripes
the bit that he washes with a whole valley he makes up
island's end   full moon still staying empty for passion

spring night fabricates a faint sweetness
the blind   make up city lights in all directions
destroyed by a candle flame that has forever lost its memory
to be kindled into the lilacs   like a tugboat towing
non–existing geography
exist   wantonly pressed tight into a dead corner
by the two upper reaches of before and after

'*river*, like *lotus*, is pronounced *ho*': Or we could do this in Latin: Flumen, sicut lilium, *ho* dicitur

这里 《水经注》本身也漂泊着
这角落漆成深蓝色时援引一声雁唳
远隔千年的一次点名 点到他他就出现了
牡蛎丛生的一本传记 不写
河也写完了 切开虎皮兰他摸到那流动
走投无路却不得不流

入 无声 肯定

鬼魂行走时趟起的片片月色是真的

here   *Waterways Classic Annotated* is drifting itself
when this corner is painted dark blue it invokes a cry from a wild goose
the roll call a thousand years away   he's called and then he appears
a biography overgrown with oysters   no writing
writing about rivers finished too   when the tiger lily is cut open he touches
that flow
no way out but still have to flow

into   soundlessness   confirm

sheets of moonlight raised when ghosts walk are real

二十一　离题诗

某一个他：水是无色的

每种颜色都是谎言　当水
忍着没完没了的一次从对岸开始
从隔开开始

每种颜色都在把这块岩石举得更高
当波涛追逐　而月光学会想像
一夜故事里头晕目眩的海拔

我们想不讲也不行　不看
漆黑的天上大群海蜇也蜇着地平线
疼　热情打捞两个坐着的形象

我的手在你身上只活一刹那
就伤了　歌手唱道　记住这四月
记着　一片溃散的银白铺满视野之外

一种黑暗的纯被吸进肺里
肉体就不怕一首诗的流向
永远更赤裸　比一捧雪或一块冰

.
还赤裸　两个海互相打湿时
两只偷听的右耳都埋进一滴古往今来的水
忍着　没人能泅渡的无色

神仙们也隔着繁星苦苦盼望相会的日子
摇荡　明知虚空的杯子
当　漏出的爱正制成一弯彩虹

21 *An off-theme verse*
A CERTAIN HE: WATER IS COLOURLESS

every colour is a lie   when water
endures one endless time and starts from the opposite shore
starts from a separation

every colour is lifting this rock higher
when breakers chase   and moonlight has learned to imagine
a dizzy elevation in stories all night long

we want to shut up but cannot   shut our eyes
in pitch-dark sky a big group of jellyfish is stinging the horizon too
pain   ardently salvages both images of sitting

my hands only survive for an instant on your body
then they're injured   vocalists sing   remember this April
remember   an expanse of routed silver-white beyond spread-out vision

a kind of dark purity is inhaled into the lungs
so the body doesn't fear the direction of a verse's flow
forever barer   compared with a handful of snow or a piece of ice
even barer   when two seas splash each other
two overhearing right ears are buried into a drop of eternal water
enduring   colourlessness that no one can swim across

beyond the stars immortals go on yearning for a reunion day too
shake   an obviously empty glass
when   the leaking out of love is being made into a rainbow

二十二　离题诗

另一个他：绿琥珀

五十万年里包含多少二十四岁的一瞬
这块绿暂停着　花朵们的一生
隐在水下　不知为谁保存的银白
不停雕成更美的残骸
绿　握在手中才感到　五十万年象
我们身上一阵止不住的颤抖

二十四个夏天分泌躲进肉里的香
我们嗅着自己死过一次的嗅觉
雨声淅沥　记起就硬了
打湿的梧桐叶和一个移开的窗口
移进　你的往事　我的往事
每天升高一寸的浸没两个名字的水位

没有诗的日子多好啊　没有
幸福　鬼魂就不必悔恨非人的冷
没有下午四点半一支阳光的针剂
我们就不等　醒的片刻中毒的片刻
没有文字　你认识我刚从伤口中
滴下来的形象

一瞥　绿的体积一页页堆满了初稿
海鸥恍若笔误的叫声　停在
天上　我的往事　你的往事
彼此想像有一条路　没走过才更晶莹
两次走过　两个会变老的宇宙
被离别保鲜的疼多好啊

被绿绿的体内抱着
一枚花瓣银闪闪地再死一次　无数枚
嗅着同一个死后　四溢的香
我们终于追上自己的颤抖时
二十四岁中写满的血肉　终于能够被忘掉
握紧　五十万年才配称为一瞬

ANOTHER HE: GREEN AMBER

five hundred thousand years include how many instants of being twenty-four
this piece of green is pausing   whole life of flowers
hidden under water   silver white kept for someone unknown
is carved non-stop into prettier skeletons
green   feel only in a hand's grip   five hundred thousand years are like
a ceaseless shiver in our bodies

twenty-four summers secret fragrance hidden in flesh
we're smelling our own sense of smell that has died once
pattering of raindrops   turns stiff in recollection
wet leaves of wutong trees and a window removed
move into   your past events   my past events
water level rising an inch everyday submerges two names

days without poetry are so good   without
happiness   ghosts don't have to regret deeply inhuman coldness
without an injection of sunshine at 4:30 P.M.
we don't wait for   a sober moment, a poisoned moment
without words   you know the image of me
dripping off a wound just now

a glimpse   volume of green piled in sheets to fill a manuscript
cries of seagulls sounding like slips of the pen   stop in
the sky   my past events   your past events
you and I imagine a road   more sparkling only if it hasn't been walked past
twice walk past   two universes that will grow old
pain preserved by a departure is so good

hugged by the green insides of a body
a petal dies once more glinting with silver   numberless petals
smelling the same post-mortem   spill of fragrance
when we catch up with our own shiver at last
flesh and blood written to fill twenty-four years of age   can be forgotten at last
hold fast   only five hundred thousand years will qualify as an instant

二十三　离题诗

某一个他：沿着自己离去

从一本书的结尾向回读
我们能与谁重逢

从　鸟儿陷进蓝蓝粘土的拍翅声
肯定　失去也是一种美

我的信抵达时　连笔迹都变了
你印刷在旧照上的别人的脸

要求一架鸟瞰的仪器　遥测
嘴角一道昨夜的裂纹

勒到肉里像假的　深及隐匿的某人时
毁灭性的真　蚌壳暗红的内部

谁知有没有历史那颗珍珠
撬开　你的耳垂听着圆润的泪

我的舌尖　被鸟头里一块磁石领着
陶醉于末日甜蜜的引力

沿着自己离去　向前　呼吸把我们挪远
向后　上溯母亲分娩的血腥运河

许多一生的昨夜　死者
玩味着抚摸那不可能的温度

许多手隐匿在皮肤下　五指腐烂
被彻底掐断的鸟鸣

彻底是一条轨迹　贯穿精雕细刻的
死也找不到的这支手

捧着一本书　从结尾读到结尾
从粉碎声　重温我们能多么温柔

106

23 *An off-theme verse*
A CERTAIN HE: LEAVE ALONG ONESELF

read backward from the end of a book
who can we meet again

from   sounds of birds stuck in blue clay and flapping their wings
sure   losing something is a kind of beauty too

when my letter arrives   even the handwriting has changed
the face of another person you printed on an old photo

ask the bird's-eye view equipment   to remote sense
the crack at a corner of the mouth last night

cut into the flesh as if it's fake   when it's deep as someone hidden
destructive reality   the dark red inside of an oyster shell

who knows if there is that pearl of history
prized   your earlobes listening to pearly tears

my tongue tip   led by a magnet inside a bird's head
revels in the sweet force of doomsday

leave along oneself   forward   breathing moves us far away
backward   go upstream along the bloody canal of mother's labour

last night of many lives   the dead
ponder as they stroke that impossible temperature

many hands hide under the skin   five rotten fingers
bird songs thoroughly nipped off

thoroughness is an orbit   to penetrate a meticulously carved
death   this hand still can't be found

hold a book in both hands   read from the end to the end
from the sound of shattering   relive how gentle we could be

二十四 离题诗

另一个他：水中

为昨天哭泣吧 但别像昨天那样哭
欲望和距离 孪生的主题
一个人展览一幅生下就灭了顶的静物
而一条河酷似对话地自言自语
说出声时 水中都是疯子

跟着落日疯 粼粼转盘上镏金的骰子
骨灰瓮 盛着黄昏天边的一把灰
用一个刚刚换下的昨天摩擦你
人称换成水 波浪那首诗
已不可能不幽暗

圆心封存当年的愚蠢
想像有个轮回 但我在哪次轮回里
掌心五根鱼骨 那洁白——磨制赝品
水下远眺又一夜洇开墨汁
沁入 疯子们语法投影的月全食

我返回 但能被哪双眼睛认出
你依稀在白发间剩下
一个现实 一滴滴煮开却从未离开的过去
海水静静改写血缘的比例
想像一个尽头吧 当尽头本身无穷无尽

当一把手术刀用切掉一天切掉我们的性
当厌倦的深 厌倦了深度
就把我当个入海口吧 没有的方向上
一场风暴在你的分界处粉红愕动
听着零点 听不见地开始

ANOTHER HE: IN THE WATER

cry for yesterday   but don't cry like yesterday
desire and distance   twin themes
a person exhibits a still life already drowned at birth
and a river talks to itself exactly like a conversation
when they speak up   everyone in the water is crazy

crazy along with the setting sun   gilded dice on a crystal turntable
cinerary urn   holds a handful of ashes on the horizon at dusk
rubs you with a yesterday that's just been replaced
persons changed into water   the wave that poem
no longer possible not to be obscure

the circle's centre seals in the stupidity of these years
imagine there's a transmigration   yet in which transmigration am I
in the palm five fish bones   that pure white polish faked one by one
under the water watching from far away the ink running all night again
seeping into   total lunar eclipse projected by the grammar of lunatics

I go back   but which pair of eyes can recognise me
you are vaguely left between white hairs
a reality   a past cooked drop by drop but never gone
seawater rewrites quietly the proportion of consanguinity
imagine an end   when the end is itself endless

when a scalpel takes one cut-off day to cut off our sex
when the depth of weariness   has wearied depth
treat me as an entrance to the sea   in the direction of zero
a storm palpitates with pink terror on your dividing line
listen to the zero point   start without hearing

二十五　离题诗

某一个他：傍晚的某座庭院

海平线隐身测量墙上这些缺口
松针之间　一把把象牙扇骨脱落
硫磺味儿中嵌着孔雀
细小的死去的步子

又一些辞　把两次交谈隔开更远
又一些时刻在这一刻里开采
鸟鸣　五点钟睡醒的空间
一枝烟袅袅搭建着　大理石拍响翅膀

又一些来历消失　呼吸
被剩下　戳着天空柔软的腹部
又是无痛的　一片蓝漏了电
一次熄灭在鉴赏中鲜美如第一次

日子这么大　足够云的断桨漂过
熏香的树木间我们坐着
早已爱上了一阵驱逐的哨音
再黑些　再拿走今夜　和几千年一起

110

25 *An off-theme verse*
GLOAMING IN SOME GARDEN

the sea's horizon invisibly inspects these gaps in the wall
fan's ivory ribs cast off one by one   among the pine needles
smell of sulphur set with peacocks
tiny dead footsteps

again words   divide two conversations still further
again more moments extracted from within this moment
birdsong   a space of waking at five P.M.
cigarette smoke curling, building up   marbles clap their wings

again more origins vanish breathing
left behind   poking the soft belly of the sky
again it's painless   a stretch of blue leaking electricity
extinguishing once in being appreciated is as fresh as the first time

the day so big   big enough to let broken oars of clouds drift by
we sit among smoke-cured trees
fallen in love long ago with a banished whistle
be darker   take tonight away again   with thousands of years